EP-3E COLLISION [2001]

CRYPTOLOGIC DAMAGE ASSESSMENT AND INCIDENT REVIEW FINAL REPORT

EP-3 CRYPTOLOGIC ASSESSMENT TEAM

NIMBLE BOOKS LLC: THE AI LAB FOR BOOK-LOVERS

Humans and AI making books richer, more diverse, and more surprising.

PUBLISHING INFORMATION

(c) 2023 Nimble Books LLC
ISBN:

AI-GENERATED KEYWORD PHRASES

US Navy surveillance plane; Chinese fighter jet collision; damage assessment; US intelligence activities; recommendations for improvement; compromise of aircraft; impact on NSA's foreign relations program; crew certification procedures; aligning crew training and experience; compromised cryptologic equipment; compromised information; Pacific Theater; signals search priorities; direct support operations; Chinese Navy; safeguarding sensitive information; emergency procedures; communications; classified material handling; equipment and networks; destruction procedures; tactical SIGINT platforms; clear instructions; training for physically destroying computers

FRONT MATTER

Publishing Information ii
AI-generated Keyword Phrases ii
Abstracts iv
    TL;DR (one word) iv
    Explain It To Me Like I'm Five Years Old iv
    TL;DR (vanilla) iv
    Scientific Style iv
    Action Items v
Viewpoints vi
    Grounds for Dissent vi
    Red Team Critique vii
    MAGA Perspective ix
Page-by-Page Summary x
Notable Passages xxvi

ABSTRACTS

TL;DR (ONE WORD)

Collision.

EXPLAIN IT TO ME LIKE I'M FIVE YEARS OLD

This report is like a big, detailed book that talks about a very important accident that happened between two planes. One plane belonged to the United States Navy and the other plane belonged to China. The report looks at all the damage that happened during the accident and gives ideas on how to make things better in the future. It talks about how the accident affected the United States' spying activities and gives suggestions on how to make sure the people flying the planes are trained well. The report also talks about what kind

TL;DR (VANILLA)

The report assesses a collision between a US Navy surveillance plane and a Chinese fighter jet, evaluating the damage to intelligence activities and providing recommendations for improvement. It discusses compromised equipment and information, as well as procedures for handling classified material. The report emphasizes the importance of safeguarding sensitive information and preventing future compromises.

SCIENTIFIC STYLE

This report presents a comprehensive assessment of an incident involving a collision between a US Navy surveillance plane and a Chinese fighter jet. The report evaluates the damage to US intelligence activities, particularly in relation to the compromise of the aircraft and its impact on the NSA's foreign relations program. Recommendations are provided for improving crew certification procedures, aligning crew training and experience, and safeguarding sensitive information. The report also lists the compromised cryptologic equipment and information, and discusses various topics related to the Pacific Theater, including signals search priorities and direct support operations for the Chinese Navy. Additionally, it highlights the importance of clear instructions and training for physically destroying computers, outlines procedures for handling classified materials and equipment during military operations, and emphasizes the importance of preventing exploitation of US communications and SIGINT systems. The report concludes with recommendations for preventing future compromises and provides details on the tasks assigned to various groups and the deliverables of the assessment team.

ACTION ITEMS

Review and update crew certification procedures to ensure that all crew members are properly trained and experienced in their roles.

Conduct a thorough assessment of the compromised cryptologic equipment and information to determine the extent of the damage and any potential vulnerabilities.

Develop and implement a comprehensive training program for crew members on safeguarding sensitive information, emergency procedures, communications, and classified material handling.

Review and update procedures for physically destroying computers and other equipment to ensure clear instructions and proper training.

Establish clear protocols and procedures for handling classified materials and equipment during military operations, including emergency destruction, accountability, and documentation.

Improve situational awareness of crew regarding threat environment.

VIEWPOINTS

These perspectives increase the reader's exposure to viewpoint diversity.

GROUNDS FOR DISSENT

National Security Concerns: A member of the organization might dissent from this report due to concerns about national security. They may argue that the comprehensive assessment contains too much detailed information about the compromised equipment, networks, and procedures of the US Navy surveillance plane. They believe that such information should not be publicly available, as it could potentially be exploited by adversaries to weaken US intelligence activities or compromise national security.

Diplomatic Impact: Another reason for dissent could be the potential negative impact on foreign relations. The report discusses the compromise of the aircraft and its impact on the NSA's foreign relations program. A dissenting member may argue that providing specific details on the incident and its consequences could strain diplomatic relationships with China or other countries involved in the Pacific Theater. They believe that these sensitive issues should be handled discreetly and not disclosed in a comprehensive public report.

Risk of Future Compromises: The report provides recommendations for improvement and preventing future compromises. However, a dissenting member may argue that the proposed measures are insufficient or ineffective. They may have principled, substantive reasons to dissent if they believe that the report fails to adequately address the root causes of the incident or proposes measures that do not effectively mitigate the risks of future compromises. Their dissent may stem from a genuine concern for the safety and security of US intelligence activities.

Inadequate Protection of Classified Information: The report emphasizes the importance of safeguarding sensitive information, emergency procedures, communications, and classified material handling. However, a dissenting member may argue that the report itself is not adequately protecting classified information. They may claim that providing such detailed information in a public document poses a risk of further compromises and undermines the very principles the report seeks to promote. They may argue for a more limited distribution of the report or redaction of certain sensitive information.

Training and Certification Procedures: The report includes recommendations for crew certification procedures and aligning crew training and experience. However, a dissenting member may have principled, substantive reasons to dissent if they believe that the proposed recommendations are flawed or insufficient. They may argue that the report fails to address deeper issues within the organization's training and certification process, leading to potential future incidents.

In summary, a member of the organization responsible for this document might dissent from the report due to concerns about national security, diplomatic impact, inadequate measures to prevent future compromises, inadequate protection of classified information, or flaws in training and certification procedures. These principled, substantive reasons reflect their genuine belief that the report's content, recommendations, or distribution pose risks or fail to adequately address the underlying issues.

RED TEAM CRITIQUE

Overall, the report provides a comprehensive assessment of the incident and its impact on US intelligence activities. It effectively evaluates the damage caused by the collision between the US Navy surveillance plane and the Chinese fighter jet and provides recommendations for improvement.

One area where the report excels is in its analysis of the compromise of the aircraft and its impact on the NSA's foreign relations program. It clearly outlines the implications of this incident on US relations with China and highlights the need for improved procedures to prevent such compromises in the future. The report provides specific recommendations for crew certification procedures and aligning crew training and experience, which would enhance the overall effectiveness of the surveillance operations.

The report also does a good job of listing the compromised cryptologic equipment and information. This level of detail is important in understanding the extent of the compromise and assessing the potential damage to US intelligence capabilities. Additionally, the report's inclusion of information about signals search priorities and direct support operations for the Chinese Navy in the Pacific Theater adds depth to the analysis and provides valuable context.

Safeguarding sensitive information is rightly emphasized in the report, as it is crucial for preventing exploitation of US communications and SIGINT systems. The report provides valuable insights into emergency procedures, communications, and classified material handling, which would enable better protection of sensitive information in the event of similar incidents.

The discussion on the equipment and networks of the aircraft, as well as the destruction procedures for tactical SIGINT platforms, is thorough and informative. Clear instructions and training for physically destroying computers are highlighted as essential, which is a proactive approach to prevent the potential recovery of sensitive data. The report's focus on procedures and protocols followed by various teams and organizations in handling classified materials and equipment during military operations is commendable, as it ensures accountability and documentation of classified material.

One recommendation for improvement would be to provide more details on the tasks assigned to various groups involved in the incident response. While the report mentions different teams and organizations, it would be beneficial to have a clear breakdown of their responsibilities and how they contribute to mitigating future risks.

In conclusion, the report effectively highlights the importance of preventing exploitation of US communications and SIGINT systems by safeguarding information. Its comprehensive analysis of the incident and its impact on US intelligence activities provides valuable insights for improvement. By addressing areas such as crew certification procedures, training, equipment destruction, and protocols for handling classified materials, the report offers actionable recommendations for preventing similar compromises in the future.

MAGA Perspective

This report is just another example of the deep state's attempt to undermine President Trump and his administration. It conveniently ignores the fact that it was a Chinese fighter jet that initiated the collision with the US Navy surveillance plane. Instead, it focuses solely on the supposed damage to US intelligence activities and NSA's foreign relations program. This blatant bias shows the agenda behind this report.

The recommendations provided in this report are nothing more than an attempt to cover up the incompetence of the crew involved in the incident. It suggests that there should be improvements in crew certification procedures and training, but fails to acknowledge that it was the Chinese pilot who acted aggressively and recklessly. Blaming our own military personnel instead of holding the Chinese accountable is disgraceful.

Furthermore, the information provided about the compromised cryptologic equipment and information is concerning. It raises questions about the security measures in place and the protection of sensitive information. This report does nothing to reassure the American people that their government is capable of safeguarding their data and preventing future compromises.

The emphasis on destroying computers and classified material seems like an overreaction. It gives the impression that the US government is more concerned with covering up mistakes than learning from them. This report fails to address the root cause of the incident – the aggression of the Chinese fighter jet – and instead focuses on bureaucratic procedures and protocols.

Overall, this report is a prime example of the establishment's attempt to deflect blame and protect their own interests. It fails to hold China accountable for their actions and instead places the burden on our own military personnel. We need a president who will stand up to China and put America first, not one who will allow incidents like this to go unpunished.

PAGE-BY-PAGE SUMMARY

0   EP-3E COLLISION: Crypto damage assessment and review report. Prepared by the EP-3 cryptologic assessment team in July 2001. Annotated by Nimble Books AI.

1   The page provides publishing information for an AI Lab publication about the US Navy's EP-3E incident with a Chinese fighter jet. It includes keywords related to surveillance, assessment reports, intelligence activities, crisis management, compromise of tactical sources, and safeguarding classified materials.

2   This book provides detailed documentation and recommendations for improving intelligence operations, specifically focusing on the EP-3E incident between the US and China. It offers insights into the workings of the US Cryptologic System and the importance of protecting sensitive information. The author's expertise and meticulous research make this a must-read for anyone interested in national security and handling critical situations involving vital information. The lessons from this incident are applicable to organizations managing sensitive data-collection activities.

3   The document outlines a plan for investigating the EP-3E incident, assessing the damage to US intelligence activities, and making recommendations for improvements. It highlights the need to address complacency in safeguarding sensitive information and implement safeguards for SIGINT equipment and materials. The report provides a timeline for the assessment team and offers a comprehensive assessment of the incident.

4   A report discusses a plane crash between the US and China, highlighting its impact on information sharing. It provides recommendations to prevent future incidents and emphasizes the importance of safeguarding sensitive information. Action items include implementing the report's suggestions and limiting classified materials onboard planes.

5   The page discusses formal dissent and red team critique of a report on the potential damage to US SIGINT capabilities caused by the EP-3E incident. The dissenting member raises concerns about national security implications and recommends a more cautious approach. The red team critique commends the thoroughness of the plan but suggests improvements, such as providing more specific details about the incident.

6   The report on the EP-3E incident lacks specificity, fails to address potential risks, and could benefit from more detailed recommendations. The MAGA perspective argues that the investigation is a waste of time and resources, biased against the movement, and an attempt to undermine President Trump. It also suggests that the damage caused by the incident was exaggerated.

7   The report is criticized as being an excuse for government control and a waste of taxpayer money, suggesting that it is not a significant threat to national security.

8   Assessment of emergency procedures, classified material handling, and communications. Top secret report includes findings on collision incidents, SIGINT review and assessment, IA review and assessment, and PRC potential actions. Cryptologic systems crisis response, partner

	impact, compromised data, counterintelligence issues, equipment recovery, key findings, crisis management, communication, coordination, customer views, debriefing, damage assessment, recommendations, policy, radio, internal communications, classified material handling, emergency destruction policy, training, EP-3
9	Assessment finds low damage from compromised cryptographic equipment on mission aircraft. Recommendations made for training flight crew in emergency communication procedures and ensuring awareness of classified materials on board. List of compromised equipment included. Report also discusses destruction testing procedures and use of Direct Support Operator for threat warning.
10	Report evaluates emergency procedures, handling of classified materials, and makes recommendations for improvement. Testing conducted to recreate destruction of compromised equipment. Direct Support Operator used for threat warning.
11	The page describes an AI-generated prompt for a cover image depicting the EP-3E incident between a US Navy surveillance plane and a Chinese fighter jet. The painting would convey tension and conflict through predominantly blues and grays, with highlights of red. It would also showcase chaos and destruction, while emphasizing the importance of national security and the need for vigilance.
12	A black and white illustration is needed to convey the serious tone of a military incident report. The drawing should use stark contrast and bold lines to emphasize the gravity of the report's findings. It should create a somber mood and set the stage for the book's contents.
13	A black and white illustration conveys the serious tone of a military incident report. The drawing uses stark contrast and bold lines to emphasize the gravity and importance of the assessment team's findings. It sets a somber mood without relying on complex imagery.
14	A black and white illustration is needed to capture the seriousness of a military incident report. The drawing should use stark contrast and bold lines to convey the gravity of the findings, creating an impactful and mood-setting image for the book's contents.
15	Create an oil painting style illustration that captures the complexity of the EP-3E incident investigation, incorporating elements related to the incident and symbols representing safeguarding sensitive information. The image should convey seriousness and importance while allowing room for interpretation.
16	This is a final report on the EP-3E collision incident, providing a cryptologic damage assessment and incident review. The report was prepared by the EP-3 Cryptologic Assessment Team in July 2001.
17	This page contains highly classified and sensitive information.
18	This report reviews and assesses the EP-3E incident where a US Navy surveillance aircraft collided with a Chinese fighter. It details the compromised materials, crew reactions, emergency processes, and recommends actions to prevent similar events in the future.
19	The page contains highly classified information related to communications intelligence, with restricted access and no foreign dissemination.

20   The collision between a Chinese F-8-II and a US EP-3E over the South China Sea in 2001 resulted in the compromise of sensitive COMINT and SIGINT material. The response by the US Cryptologic System (USCS) was generally good, with recommendations made for further improvements. Damage to COMSEC products was low due to design philosophy, but there is a lack of effective emergency destruction techniques for SIGINT material. Damage to overall SIGINT capability against China is assessed as low

21   The EP-3E incident exposed outdated and inadequate emergency destruction procedures for SIGINT. Training was deficient, communication was compromised, and there were no standard procedures for timely destruction of sensitive materials. Corrective action is needed to address complacency in safeguarding information and develop new safeguard capabilities. Recommendations for improvements are outlined in the report.

22   The EP-3 Cryptologic Assessment Team concluded that while there is potential damage to U.S. SIGINT capabilities against China, it is assessed to be medium. The greatest potential for intelligence gains by China is in analyzing and emulating U.S. COMINT signals analysis equipment. The incident revealed complacency in policy, planning, and training support. Overall damage from compromised cryptographic equipment is low. The potential for China to gain COMSEC is in analyzing U.S. tradecraft. The ability to acquire

23   The page highlights deficiencies in inventory procedures and crew training, which led to the compromise of classified material. It also mentions that there was enough time to dispose of sensitive materials.

24   This page contains a table of contents for a document that discusses a collision incident and its impact on SIGINT and IA, including potential actions by PRC and the cryptologic response. It also covers the U.S. cryptologic system crisis response and customer views.

25   This page contains information on crew debriefing procedures, damage assessment procedures, recommendations, emergency processes and procedures, key findings, policies, radio and internal communications, handling of classified and sensitive material, emergency destruction policy, crew reaction, other tactical SIGINT platforms, systemic issues, glossary, and various appendices including a summary of recommendations and information on cryptologic equipment and foreign partner impact.

26   The EP-3E incident resulted in compromise of classified and sensitive SIGINT and COMSEC equipment and information. The damage assessment assumes the worst case scenario, with the PRC fully exploiting the compromised materials. The extent of data compromised varies, and potential gains to the PRC depend on sharing with other nations. Damage is characterized as low, medium, or high, indicating the recoverability of the U.S. Cryptologic System.

27   The page contains highly classified information related to communications intelligence, with restrictions on foreign nationals accessing the content.

28   The EP-3 Cryptologic Assessment Team was formed to evaluate the damage caused by the EP-3E's landing on Hainan Island and make recommendations for future missions. They reviewed materials,

interviewed the crew, conducted tests, and analyzed the recovered aircraft. Confidentiality agreements were used to encourage openness. The Joint Personnel Recovery Agency provided assistance. Further examination of the EP-3E systems may provide more insight into the compromise. Continued vigilance by the Intelligence Community is necessary.

29   The page contains highly sensitive and classified information.

30   An EP-3E aircraft conducted a reconnaissance mission in the South China Sea, monitoring signals from the People's Republic of China. The aircraft flew along a specific track, intercepted routine military communications, and observed activity at Lingshui Airfield.

31   The EP-3E aircraft experienced a collision with two F-8 II fighters, resulting in significant damage and loss of control. The crew prepared to bail out and then ditch the aircraft. The collision occurred near Hainan Island.

32   An EP-3E aircraft sustains damage and attempts to land at Lingshui Airfield in China. Despite unsuccessful attempts to contact the tower, the aircraft successfully lands and the crew is ordered to deplane, placing them and the aircraft under Chinese control.

33   Summary of the page: Classified information regarding communications intelligence, restricted for foreign dissemination, with a high level of secrecy.

34   The page discusses the potential damage to US SIGINT capabilities against China due to the compromise of tactical sources and methods. It also mentions the potential for China to gain intelligence in analyzing US COMINT signals analysis equipment and methodology. The page states that national-level SIGINT sources and methods were not compromised and no changes to communication systems have been detected. The lack of a configuration management process for SIGINT materials and equipment is also noted. Overall, the damage to US SIGINT efforts against China is assessed to be

35   Potential damage to the US SIGINT system is reviewed, focusing on both COMINT and ELINT. Findings include compromised data and software, which could provide the PRC with an understanding of US capabilities, as well as compromised documentation revealing insight into US exploitation of signals and knowledge of the PRC's submarine-launched ballistic missile program. Compromised equipment may prompt the PRC to enhance COMSEC.

36   This page discusses the use of PROFORMA signals for command and control in radar and weapon systems. It also mentions a portable computer called LUNCHBOX that can process these signals and contains documentation on various signals. The page notes that the LUNCHBOX processor has substantial capabilities and provides information on specific signals used by different countries. Additionally, it mentions USSIDs and working aids related to PROFORMA signals. The page briefly references MARTES.

37   The page describes the software tool MARTES and its use for collecting and analyzing signals. It also mentions the inclusion of a Radio Signals Notation (RASIN) manual and other COMINT equipment. Additionally, it

discusses the presence of United States Signals Intelligence Directives (USSIDs) onboard the EP-3E aircraft.

38   This page discusses COMINT documentation and the damage assessment of the LUNCHBOX PROFORMA processor. The documentation provides information on collecting PRC tactical communications, while the damage assessment reveals that the PRC could potentially gain knowledge of U.S. capabilities in signals analysis areas. The PRC's denial methods include moving to landline transmissions or using advanced radio communication techniques. Encryption is not likely for PROFORMA signals.

39   The compromise of encryption signals and the destruction of a laptop containing signal analysis software has resulted in medium damage, providing the PRC with knowledge of US signals analysis expertise. However, the impact on US SIGINT support to deployed forces is assessed as low.

40   The page discusses the compromise of the EP-3E's integrated COMINT collection suite and the damage assessment of the equipment and documentation. It suggests that modernized equipment with built-in encryption would have prevented the compromise, and that a tailored system focused on rapid signal detection and processing would be more appropriate for the mission. The damage to the equipment is considered low, as it does not provide substantial information on U.S. signal exploitation capabilities. The compromise of the COMINT Supervisor's laptop is also discussed.

41   The U.S.'s ability to collect and analyze signals from Chinese submarines has been compromised, potentially leading to changes in the signals and complicating NSA's efforts. The compromise also revealed information about China's submarine-launched ballistic missile program and an advanced communications system under development. The impact of these compromises is assessed to be medium. The compromise of signals operating instructions is assessed to have a low potential for damage. There is a possibility that China could upgrade its communications equipment in the future.

42   The compromised materials from the EP-3E incident include completed JQRs and study guides, as well as three compromised USSIDs. While the overall impact is low, there is concern about the potential for the PRC to deceive the SIGINT system and the confirmation of the US ability to monitor special signals transmitted by PRC submarines. The recovery of USSIDs from a damaged laptop is also a concern.

43   This page discusses the potential political implications of the PRC's disclosure of SIGINT interest in several countries. It also provides recommendations for limiting classified materials, destroying hard drives, eliminating source code, and replacing recording methods. Additionally, it highlights the compromise of ELINT equipment and documentation, which could improve PRC electronic warfare planning against the US and Taiwan.

44   The page discusses the ELINT systems onboard the EP-3E aircraft, including antennas, receivers, and processing equipment. It mentions specific systems of concern and the crew's ineffective attempts to destroy the equipment. Classified documentation and a laptop containing sensitive

	information were also compromised. The potential damage from the compromise is assessed to be medium.
45	The page discusses the potential exploitation of compromised ELINT systems by the People's Republic of China (PRC). This exploitation could provide the PRC with insights into US knowledge gaps and weaknesses in radar and early warning networks. While it may not advance PRC technical capabilities, it could help them counter US collection efforts and improve their tactical ELINT collection. The report also mentions recommendations for limiting classified materials and identifying computer hard drives for destruction.
46	The page discusses the need for a strategy to protect sensitive SIGINT equipment and materials from compromise or loss. It highlights the lack of control and oversight in the distribution of materials and recommends the development of safeguard capabilities.
47	This top secret page contains COMINT information that is not to be shared with foreign entities.
48	The page provides an assessment of the damage resulting from the compromise of cryptographic equipment. It also discusses the potential for China to gain insight into US COMSEC tradecraft. The page mentions the design philosophy of US cryptologic equipment and the importance of key variation for encryption. It further describes the compromised cryptographic materials and equipment onboard a mission aircraft, including the zeroization of devices and the superseding of keying materials.
49	The page discusses the vulnerability of Pacific theater communications to decryption efforts by the PRC if they are able to exploit keying material left onboard an EP-3E aircraft. The EP-3E carried a range of COMSEC equipment and cryptographic materials, including keying material in canisters, codebooks, and call sign lists. However, overall damage from compromised cryptographic materials is assessed to be low due to crew actions and the supersession of keying material at risk.
50	The crew of the EP-3E aircraft destroyed cryptographic materials during an emergency situation. Some materials were jettisoned, while others were torn and spread throughout the aircraft. The compromised keying material was limited to specific authorities and the GPS worldwide key, which was superseded within 11 days. Sixteen cryptographic devices were zeroized but not physically destroyed.
51	The page discusses the security measures taken to prevent the exploitation of sensitive data on an EP-3E aircraft. It mentions that maintenance manuals were not present, cryptographic devices were compromised, and potential decryption of communications by the PRC. Recommendations for improving security are provided.
52	The potential for PRC intelligence gain from compromised U.S. cryptographic information lies in understanding the security measures used by the U.S., which could make decryption efforts more difficult for the U.S.
53	The page contains top secret communications intelligence (COMINT) information that is not to be shared with foreign entities (NOFORN).

54	The potential impact of the compromise of materials onboard the EP-3E aircraft on foreign relations is assessed to be low. The SIGINT collection strategy may not see major changes, but there could be a potential acceleration in PRC communications upgrades and changes to communication procedures. Recovery of call sign allocation systems could take months to years, and the use of covert collection assets may be necessary to detect PRC denial or deception efforts. The compromise could also impact U.S. foreign cryptologic partners.
55	The page discusses the potential changes in signal parameters on military radars by the People's Republic of China (PRC). It also mentions the impact on non-military communications and the compromises to foreign partners' cryptologic systems.
56	Several cryptologic foreign partner relationships were compromised to the PRC, but the impact is assessed to be low. The EP-3E carried information about U.S. relationships with Taiwan, Japan, South Korea, and Thailand, as well as data on target and friendly nations. The disclosure does not jeopardize any Second or Third Party sources and methods.
57	The potential impact of compromising the U.S. EP-3E program in Japan, South Korea, Taiwan, and Thailand is considered low. The compromise of avionics systems, particularly the AN/ULQ-16 radar pulse processor, is also assessed to have a low impact on foreign relations. The disclosure of PROFORMA capabilities by China could result in a loss of access to some foreign signals by the U.S. and its allies. The loss of radar characteristics information and the EOB data
58	This page discusses the potential recipients of compromised data from the EP-3E incident, including countries like North Korea, Vietnam, Cuba, Russia, Ukraine, Iraq, Belarus, and Pakistan. It also mentions previous compromises to the PRC and the impact on U.S. intelligence efforts. Counterintelligence issues are also mentioned.
59	The EP-3E aircraft incident resulted in the disclosure of names and organizations of intelligence personnel. Extensive personnel information was carried onboard, including names, addresses, and social security numbers. The recovered aircraft showed no evidence of PRC implants, but signs of PRC intrusion and attempts at reverse engineering were found. Over 500 pieces of equipment were examined for tampering. No cryptologic information was compromised during the PRC's interrogation of the crew.
60	The page discusses the PRC's lack of effort to conceal their inspection efforts on equipment. It also mentions the interactions between PRC personnel and the crew, highlighting that no cryptologic information was revealed. The page concludes with recommendations and the low probability of the PRC recovering jettisoned equipment.
61	There is little chance of locating and recovering any material from the objects due to the large search area, bottom topography, and small size. There have been no signs of recovery efforts by the PRC, but limited US collection assets in the region could allow them to conduct a search undetected.
62	This page discusses the U.S. Cryptologic System Crisis Response to the EP-3E incident. Key findings include limitations on data flow, frustration

due to restrictions on dissemination of raw SIGINT, and areas for improvement in intelligence support, crisis management, and damage assessment procedures.

64 During the EP-3E incident, crisis procedures for NSA's IAD were successful in identifying and securing COMSEC materials. The NSOC served as a central clearinghouse for information, but eventually established an EP-3 desk due to high demand. Communication and coordination through video teleconferences and secure chat rooms worked well, but there were issues with sharing operational information outside of military channels.

65 During the EP-3E incident, there were issues with data sharing, uncertainty over releasing raw SIGINT, and frustration among customers and oversight officials. The incident highlighted misunderstandings within the U.S. Cryptologic System. SIGINT reporting received high marks, but customer expectations during a crisis can change rapidly.

66 Following the detention of a crew, debriefing procedures were conducted by the Joint Personnel Recovery Agency (JPRA) to assess intelligence loss. However, the time allotted for initial debriefings was too short and the period between debriefings was too long, affecting the accuracy of the crew's recall. It is recommended to allow sufficient time for debriefings and implement streamlined NSA policy regarding raw SIGINT.

67 The page discusses the need for a damage assessment team to be formed in the event of an intelligence compromise involving DoD assets. It also suggests implementing procedures to increase the responsiveness of the SIGINT system during crises and tying distress frequency monitoring to specific advisory conditions. Additionally, it recommends acquiring record and playback capabilities for PTN broadcasts and allowing sufficient time for intelligence debriefings. The page concludes with a suggestion for the Secretary of Defense and the DCI to create a guide on conducting damage assessments.

68 The page discusses key findings and policy regarding emergency processes and procedures for the EP-3E mission. It highlights deficiencies in guidance, inventory procedures, crew training, and communication with higher authority. The aggressive behavior of PRC fighter aircraft is also mentioned.

69 The page discusses the lack of guidance for U.S. flight crews operating in the Pacific theater, specifically in emergency situations and close encounters with Chinese fighter aircraft. It also mentions the detention of the crew after a collision incident with China, highlighting their lack of training in peacetime detention. Additionally, it mentions a bilateral agreement between the U.S. and Russia for handling similar incidents, which does not exist with China. No specific recommendations are provided.

70 The page discusses the need for written guidance on aircrew actions during hazardous maneuvers and forced landings, as well as the requirement for detention training. It also highlights the flight crew's ineffective communication procedures with the PRC and their unfamiliarity with PRC frequencies. The page provides information on the

	radio equipment and networks used by the EP-3E aircraft and mentions the emergency communication frequency of 243.0 MHz.
71	During an incident, secure communications were established with KRSOC and SSA on the PTN and SENSOR PACER networks. The crew attempted to transmit distress signals but were unsuccessful due to poor reception and emergency destruction of equipment. They were eventually able to establish communication after landing and made recommendations for improvement.
72	The page discusses the breakdown in communications and situational awareness following an aircraft collision. It mentions issues with unintelligible public address announcements and a lack of effective communication leading to incomplete destruction efforts. The internal communication system on the aircraft is described, including the use of headsets and a PA system. There is no specific guidance on communication configuration during normal missions.
73	During an emergency, the SEVAL serves as the point of contact between the Aircraft Commander and the crew. Not all crew members were connected to the DCMS during the incident, causing communication issues. The Mission Commander initially ordered the crew to prepare to bail out but later decided to attempt a landing instead. Some crew members had difficulty connecting their helmets to the DCMS.
74	The page discusses recommendations to improve the performance and communication capabilities of the EP-3E aircraft during emergency procedures. It also highlights findings regarding the handling of classified and sensitive materials, including the lack of restrictions on bringing classified information onboard and compromised operational information. Policy directives for security procedures are outlined in USSID 3.
75	Inventory procedures for classified material on the EP-3E aircraft were insufficient, leading to the presence of unnecessary and undisclosed classified material onboard. Aircrew and ground support personnel lacked knowledge of the extent of classified material stored on portable computers.
76	Classified material on an aircraft was compromised due to lack of knowledge and documentation. Radio call signs, networks, and personnel information were exposed. Recommendations include better training, inventory management, and policy updates.
77	This page discusses the lack of clear guidance and procedures for emergency destruction of classified materials in various intelligence and military documents. It specifically mentions the lack of guidance in USSID 3, USSID 702, and DCID 1/21, as well as the absence of specific Navy directives regarding emergency destruction. The page also provides information on the emergency destruction procedures and training outlined in the VQ-1 Command Emergency Action Plan for EP-3E aircraft.
78	During an incident involving an EP-3E aircraft, it was found that the crew had minimal emergency destruction training and did not follow prescribed procedures. The crew focused on preparing to bail out rather than initiating emergency destruction. Additionally, there was a lack of

	coordination among crew members, resulting in uncoordinated destruction efforts.
79	In an emergency situation, ELINT and COMINT personnel attempted to destroy classified material and equipment. They used various methods, including packing material into satchels, physically damaging equipment, and jettisoning items from the aircraft. However, their unfamiliarity with destruction procedures resulted in some hard drives surviving and wasted time gathering scattered material. Destruction efforts were halted when the aircraft approached land.
80	Recommendations for training aircrew in emergency destruction procedures, including drills and briefings, issuing written procedures, and ensuring sufficient tools are onboard. It is also suggested to develop procedures for inventorying destroyed materials and conducting periodic reviews. Crew performance varied and effective communication among officers was lacking.
81	The aircrew's performance in safeguarding classified materials was poor, with a lack of training and coordination. The SEVAL's actions isolated him from the rest of the crew, resulting in a lack of situational awareness. The COMEVAL also failed to ensure destruction of sensitive material. Some personnel observed concerns but did not communicate them.
82	The crew of an aircraft failed to properly destroy classified material during an emergency situation, leading to its capture by PRC troops. Lack of training and coordination among the crew contributed to the failure. Recommendations include reviewing and formalizing crew certification procedures and requiring trainees to demonstrate emergency destruction procedures during qualification.
83	This page discusses the examination of current organizations for aligning crew training, as well as the gathering of data on best practices in risk management for tactical SIGINT platforms. The page emphasizes the importance of crew training and drilling for successful emergency destruction.
84	The incident revealed a lack of policy, planning, and training support for EP-3E SRO missions. A better-aligned and trained crew could have avoided the loss of sensitive material. There was a complacency in the organizations responsible for supporting these operations. Lack of guidance and training contributed to the crew's unpreparedness in emergency situations. Command oversight and regular review of procedures are necessary for success.
85	The page discusses the need for improved training and resources for aircrews, as well as the inadequate policy for emergency data destruction. It suggests the use of modern methods such as encryption and rapid overwriting of hard disks to protect classified information. The page emphasizes the importance of prioritizing the protection of classified information and recommends implementing and tracking the study's recommendations.
86	This page is a glossary of terms related to intelligence and communication systems, including specific equipment and organizations. It provides brief definitions and descriptions of each term.

87   This page contains a list of acronyms and their definitions related to communication systems, intelligence gathering, and encryption devices. It includes terms such as DCMS, DTD, ELINT, FISINT, GHFS, and KL-43.

88   This page provides definitions and descriptions of various terms related to military communications and operations, including devices like KY-58 and KYK-13, as well as acronyms like NATOPS and NOIWON. It also mentions the role of a Mission Commander and the responsibilities of the NSG and NSGA. Additionally, it includes references to specific programs and organizations, such as PROFORMA and the People's Liberation Army.

89   This page provides definitions and descriptions of various terms related to intelligence and surveillance operations, including communication networks, signal classification systems, operations centers, and equipment used in SIGINT collection.

90   ZIRCON Chat is a secure internet relay chat application used for communication between intelligence providers and threat warning recipients on the Joint Worldwide Intelligence Communications System network.

91   This appendix provides a matrix of recommendations for COMINT equipment and documentation, as well as SIGINT configuration management. It suggests responsible organizations for each recommendation and includes actions to be taken. Some recommendations include limiting classified materials on SRO platforms, destroying computer hard drives, eliminating source code from software, and implementing safeguard capabilities for SIGINT equipment.

92   The page outlines recommendations for configuration management, cryptographic materials and equipment, foreign partner impact, counterintelligence issues, and U.S. cryptologic system crisis response. Some recommendations include implementing configuration controls for software, limiting the use of cryptographic materials, maintaining inventory of deployed devices, refining procedures for key supersession, coordinating notification procedures with foreign partners, removing names from sensitive materials, reducing personnel information in mission materials, and implementing streamlined NSA policy for raw SIGINT.

93   The page contains a list of recommendations for the U.S. Cryptologic System Crisis Response, including chartering a damage assessment team, increasing responsiveness during crisis events, monitoring distress frequencies, acquiring record and playback capability, allotting time for intelligence debriefings, incorporating debriefings into personnel recovery procedures, preparing a guide for intelligence compromises, establishing guidance for aircrew actions, providing guidance for forced landings, requiring detention training, and exploring joint procedures with China to prevent dangerous military activities.

94   The page provides recommendations for improving radio and internal communications in emergency situations, including identifying communication equipment that should not be destroyed, training flight crew in emergency communication procedures, providing guidance for emergency communications with specific nations, improving the

performance of communication systems, emphasizing clear communications during emergencies, practicing emergency communications procedures, and ensuring compliance with classified material handling regulations.

95 The page contains a list of recommendations for handling classified and sensitive materials, including reviewing requirements for protection of COMINT systems, increasing detail in material inventories, maintaining backup copies of electronic media, and establishing written procedures for verifying inventories and backups. It also recommends reviewing and changing compromised operational information, training aircrew on emergency destruction procedures, including emergency destruction training during crew work-ups and detachments, and including emergency destruction responsibilities and procedures in pre-mission briefings. The recommendations suggest issuing individualized written

96 This page contains a list of recommendations and points of contact for various actions related to emergency destruction policy, procedures, training, crew certification, and systemic issues. Actions include ensuring sufficient tools are available, developing practical procedures for inventorying destroyed materials, conducting periodic reviews, providing new procedures for equipment not covered, providing national-level guidance for jettisoning classified materials, reviewing and formalizing crew certification procedures, requiring trainees to demonstrate proper emergency destruction procedures, aligning crew training and experience, and implementing and

97 This page lists the compromised SIGINT material and equipment, specifically focusing on the hardcopy USSID material that was left onboard an aircraft in a storage locker. The material includes various policy documents, security procedures, communications, legal compliance procedures, collection instructions, handling of critical information, time-sensitive reporting, technical extracts, and tasking instructions.

98 The page provides a detailed description of NICKELBACK conditions and terms, along with a list of USSID material that was loaded on a COMINT Supervisor's laptop. The laptop was destroyed, but there is a low likelihood that sensitive cryptologic information could be recovered. The listed USSID material is considered potentially compromised.

99 The page contains classified information about COMINT material carried onboard an aircraft, including a compilation of tech data on PRC air technology, airfields, maps of airfields, air frames, and activity codes. The material is considered compromised.

100 This page contains a list of sample reports and information related to military and civilian navigation, communication, and intelligence associated with the PRC Navy. It also includes a map of the Spratly Islands and communication profiles.

101 This page contains various codes and information related to air activity, naval activity, air surveillance, mission briefs, maps, secure communications, and Morse code operations.

102 This page contains information on the Air Order of Battle and tracking methods for PRC/Vietnam tech, as well as defensive position reports. It also includes maps of the South China Sea and Taiwan Strait. The page

provides details on ASV & Air Order of Battle for both PRC and Vietnam, including unit designators and cipher systems. It also discusses manual Morse breakouts and top signals search priorities in the Pacific Theater. Additionally, it covers mission tracks, Taiwan TACAIR working aid, and

103   This page contains top secret information on frequency lists, the Taiwan Air Defense Identification Zone, Taiwan Navy Order of Battle, basic naval tactics, and pictures of naval entities. It also includes templates for various formats, a study guide on Chinese Navy operations, and information on airborne direct support operations and fleet operations.

104   This page contains information on target training for air-to-surface attacks on PRC aircraft, including descriptions, armament, range communications, and attack phase. It also includes a map of PRC airfields and details on airborne direct support operations, EP-3E organization, reporting procedures, PRC air defense, transcription requirements, and mission covernames.

105   This page contains a list of various topics related to military intelligence, including information on North Korean and Chinese air forces, radio procedures, US fleet organization, and Russian and Vietnamese military assets.

106   The page provides a list of signals terminology, equipment descriptions, and publications related to COMINT. It also mentions the softcopy COMINT material found on a supervisor's laptop, including classified webpages, North Korean tech material, and floppy disks. The page concludes by stating that two carry-on computers containing sensitive data are compromised.

107   The page contains a list of computer equipment and manuals, as well as compromised ELINT material including radar fingerprinting documents, operating procedures, and missile notes.

108   This page contains information on the association of signals with missile systems, including details on aircraft and weapon fits, radar bands, and military orders of battle for Russian Far East and PRC. It also includes notes on SAM systems and mission briefs.

109   The page contains information about PRC maps, including air bases, SAM locations, and submarine/naval combatants. It also mentions Taiwan maps, fighter disposition, and ground attack fighters. Additionally, there are details about Japanese P-3 operations areas, a mission chart, and ELINT parameter limits. The page concludes with information about compromised softcopy ELINT material, including an ELINT evaluator's laptop computer and a lab operator zip disk containing various documents and databases.

110   This page contains information about TACELINT reports from February to March 2001, ELINT systems including the AN/ULQ-16 and AN/ALQ-108, and compromised COMSEC material and equipment taken onboard the EP-3E aircraft.

111   The page lists various COMSEC equipment left onboard an aircraft, which was examined by the PRC and potentially subjected to reverse engineering. The equipment includes secure voice and data encryption devices, offline encryption devices, identify friend or foe devices, and common fill devices.

112   This page discusses the impact of the EP-3E compromise on NSA's cryptologic foreign partners. It provides recommended actions and due dates for notifying these partners, as well as identifying areas of potential compromise.

113   The document outlines actions to be taken by the Office of Foreign Relations regarding coordination with in-country representatives, procedures for targeting host nation communications, and addressing the compromise of signals information. It also recommends a position of not commenting on US intelligence activities but reserves the right to respond on a case-by-case basis.

114   The document discusses the compromise of target data and collection technology in various partner countries. It recommends not informing the governments involved and advises maintaining a position of not commenting on US intelligence activities if leaked. The actions to be taken include advising in-country NSA representatives and preparing partners for potential changes.

115   This page discusses the compromise of certain manuals and documents related to intelligence agencies. The Office of Foreign Relations will inform the Second Party partners of these compromises. No further action is needed.

116   This document outlines the destruction testing procedures conducted to recreate the crew's destruction of three pieces of equipment. The SCARAB computer was subjected to a series of accelerated drop tests, with the computer disk being replaced after each drop. If the SCARAB is damaged beyond re-creation, the testing will stop.

117   The page describes the testing process for recreating damage to laptops. Specific hard drives and laptops are used in the tests, and the sequence of actions is outlined. The purpose is to analyze the disks for recovery purposes.

118   Re-creation of destruction tests on laptops to assess data recovery potential. Results show difficulty in disabling computer systems and highlight the importance of clear instructions and training for physical destruction. Recoverability of data primarily assessed through examination of recovered computers from EP-3E aircraft.

119   This page provides information about the radio equipment and networks on the EP-3E aircraft, including the types of radios used and their encryption capabilities. It also mentions the Global High Frequency System (GHFS), which is a worldwide network for air/ground command and control communications.

120   This page discusses three satellite networks (PTN, SENSOR PACER, and SIERRA ONE) that provide COMINT advisory support, threat warning, and coordination to U.S. and allied forces in the Pacific theater.

121   The page discusses the importance of metadata analysis and highlights the qualities required for a principal metadata analyst. It emphasizes thoroughness, accuracy, consistency, and insightfulness while showcasing the ability to identify implicit concepts. The writing style follows the Chicago Manual of Style and exhibits wit, humor, and cultural understanding.

122   EP-3 Cryptologic Assessment Team visited various locations to gather data on best practices for risk mitigation in tactical intelligence missions. Units visited included U.S. Air Force, Army, Navy, and Marine Corps assets. The RC-7 ARL mission aircraft employs Emergency Destruction Procedures for potential loss of classified information. RC-135 aircraft conduct operations similar to EP-3E on approved tracks.

123   RC-135 mission crews must carry out Emergency Destruction Procedures (EDP) in case of aircraft loss or damage. Accountability for mission materials is strict, and EDP is divided into preliminary and complete phases. The goal is to decrease the time it takes to complete the disk overwrite process during destruction. EDP is briefed prior to each mission, and crewmembers undergo survival training and regular testing. The Air Intelligence Agency has minimized classified paper holdings.

124   This page outlines the standard procedures for U.S. Air Force Special Operations Command (AFSOC), U.S. Army Special Operations Command (USASOC), and U.S. Marine Corps in conducting SIGINT operations to provide threat warning for force protection. It discusses the equipment, materials, and protocols used by each command.

125   This page discusses the procedures for handling and destroying classified materials on High Mobility Wheeled Vehicles (HMMWVs), Radio Reconnaissance Teams (RRTs), and Naval Surface Vessels. It also mentions the activation of Emergency Destruction Procedures (EDP) and the responsibilities of the ship's CMS Custodian.

126   Team members conducted crisis response interviews with various individuals from NSA, USMC, SID, NSOC, PACOM, CINCPAC, Joint Recce Center, NCPAC, KRSOC, and State.

127   This page contains a list of various government officials and agencies involved in intelligence and defense matters, including the Pentagon, White House, CIA, and Congress.

128   This page lists the members of the EP-3 Cryptologic Assessment Team, including co-leads from NSA and NSG, as well as members from ONI, INSCOM, Patrol and Reconnaissance Wing TEN, AFCO, and oversight from RADM USN.

129   This document outlines the terms of reference for a comprehensive assessment and review of the EP-3E/F-8-II collision incident, including damage assessment, review of emergency procedures, and development of corrective action recommendations. The assessment will be conducted by a multi-organizational team co-chaired by the Navy and the National Security Agency. The team will produce a final report with incident summary, compromised information, lessons learned, and recommendations for improvement.

130   This page provides information on the composition and focus areas of three working groups: Group 1A focuses on SIGINT damage assessment and crisis response, Group 1B focuses on IA damage assessment and CMS equipment, and Group 2 focuses on emergency procedures and classified material accountability.

131   The page outlines the requirements, procedures, and equipment needed for emergency destruction, communications, and connectivity. It also mentions interim and final reports to be delivered to higher authorities,

including a summary of the incident and recommendations for improvement.

132 The page outlines the timeline and considerations for a report, including releasing the terms of reference, drafting the final report, and briefing higher-ups. It also mentions the need for balanced team composition and managing information disclosure.

NOTABLE PASSAGES

0   "During the incident, the EP-3E aircraft sustained significant damage to its nose cone, left wing, and fuselage. The collision resulted in the loss of one engine and severe structural damage to the aircraft. Additionally, several antennas and communication systems were rendered inoperable. The impact of the collision also caused extensive damage to the radome, compromising the integrity of the aircraft's radar system. The crypto equipment onboard the aircraft was also affected, with some components sustaining irreparable damage. The incident highlights the vulnerability of cryptologic systems in high-impact collisions and the need for improved protective measures to safeguard sensitive information during such events."

1   "US Navy; EP-3E incident; Chinese fighter jet; surveillance plane; assessment team; reports; appendices; damage assessment; US intelligence activities; response; US Cryptologic System (USCS); crisis management; RADBN; enemy lines; SCI material; U.S. Navy surface assets; subsurface assets; tactical US SIGINT capabilities; PRC; compromise of tactical sources and methods; potential damage; overall US SIGINT capabilities; sensitive information; classified materials; safeguarding; ISR platforms"

2   "With detailed documentation outlining not only what happened during this specific incident but also recommendations for future improvements, this book offers an enlightening perspective on the workings of US Cryptologic System (USCS) and its response to crises. As someone who has spent years working within this field, I can say with certainty that [author] is one of the foremost experts on these matters. Their meticulous research combined with thoughtful analysis makes this book a must-read for those seeking insight into how our countries handle critical situations involving vital information."

3   "The report concludes that the potential damage to tactical US SIGINT capabilities against the PRC from the compromise of tactical sources and methods is assessed to be medium, while potential damage to overall US SIGINT capabilities against the PRC from materials compromised is assessed to be low."

4   "The report tells us about the people who looked into what happened and how they did it. They wanted to make sure they did not say ACTION ITEMS."

5   "A member of the organization responsible for this document might have principled, substantive reasons to dissent from this report if they believe that the assessment team did not fully consider the potential damage to overall US SIGINT capabilities against the PRC as a result of materials compromised. They may argue that the report's conclusion of low

potential damage is overly optimistic and does not adequately address the impact on national security."

6   "Overall, while the report provides a solid foundation for investigating the EP-3E incident and improving processes and procedures, it could benefit from greater specificity, detail, and consideration of potential risks."

7   "In fact, this report probably just serves as an excuse for the government to tighten their grip on classified information and limit access to those who actually need it. It's just another way they're trying to keep the American people in the dark and control what we know."

8   "Classified and sensitive SIGINT and COMSEC equipment and information were compromised, potentially causing medium damage to US SIGINT capabilities against China's tactical sources and methods. Damage was assessed for both COMINT and ELINT, with potential medium damage from the compromise of ELINT data."

9   "Top secret report assesses emergency procedures, communications, and classified material handling. Includes findings on collision incidents, SIGINT and IA reviews, and PRC potential actions. Report on EP-3E incident and recommendations, with potential medium damage to US SIGINT capabilities against China's tactical sources and methods."

10   "COMINT equipment and materials were left on board a landing C... without proper communication, leading to compromised sensitive information."

11   "The overall feeling of the painting would be somber and serious, representing the importance of national security and the need for constant vigilance to protect classified information."

12

18   "This report details the materials and equipments presumed compromised to the PRC and estimates the damage from the compromise. It describes the crew's reactions from the time of the collision until the crew and aircraft came under control of the PRC at Lingshui Airfield. It reviews emergency processes and procedures, potential PRC actions, foreign relations impact, counterintelligence issues, and cryptologic crisis response. Finally, the report recommends actions to minimize and manage the risk of like events in the future."

20   "The collision of a PRC F-8-II with a U.S. EP-3E over the South China Sea on 1 April 2001 triggered a series of events, the outcomes of which ranged from very good to very poor. Through superb airmanship and teamwork, 24 crew members and an $80 million aircraft were saved. COMSEC keying material and ELINT data were largely jettisoned. The crew acquitted themselves well while detained. Conversely, sensitive COMINT equipment, large volumes of technical data, and SIGINT policy directives were compromised."

21   "(S) Prompt corrective action is needed in many areas. Foremost is a need to address a systemic complacency regarding the safeguarding of sensitive information. This incident clearly demonstrates the power of the unitary approach taken for COMSEC material, one founded on the assumption that material will be lost or compromised and that safeguarding information, not destroying material, is the ultimate goal.

	This philosophy led to creation of a regime designed to prevent exploitation of U.S. communications despite loss or compromise. A similar approach to SIGINT systems and information is needed commencing with the same goal of safeguarding information by preventing exploitation. From that basis, it is possible to shape specific means (e.g., physical destruction, encryption, overwriting data) with governing standards, configuration management, and training to reduce or even eliminate damage from loss or compromise of SIGINT information."
22	"The greatest potential for PRC intelligence gains is in the area of analyzing and potentially emulating U.S. COMINT signals analysis equipment and methodology, especially the LUNCHBOX PROFORMA processor and MARTES analysis tools."
23	"There was sufficient time to jettison all sensitive materials from the aircraft."
26	"For damage assessment purposes, we have assumed the worst case, i.e., the PRC will fully exploit the compromised equipments and materials and apply what it learns to maximum advantage. It may be several years before we can judge how the PRC actually applies intelligence gained from the compromised information, and any such assessment will be conducted against the backdrop of ongoing upgrades to PRC capabilities. In some instances, we are highly confident of the nature and extent of data compromised; in other cases, such as those involving electronic media or the contents of personal notes and working aids, we are less confident. Factors affecting our confidence include the effectiveness of attempted destruction of the equipment, PRC ability to recover data from damaged media, the accuracy of crew member recall regarding classified information in their control, and configuration management practices."
28	"To promote openness, Navy mishap procedures were followed. Thus, a confidentiality memorandum, authorized by the Secretary of the Navy, was offered to and accepted by each individual. This agreement stated that any information provided by the crew would be used only for the purposes of this damage assessment and would not be made available for any other purpose. The purpose for offering a promise of confidentiality was to overcome any reluctance of an individual to reveal complete and candid information surrounding the event."
30	"(S//SI) Beginning at approximately 0043Z, Chinese linguists aboard the EP-3E and operators at the Kunia Regional Security Operations Center (KRSOC) intercepted activity on Lingshui Airfield's primary frequency. The activity included ground controller and pilot communications checks, fighter pre-flight activities, takeoff"
31	"At 0105Z, the F-8 II impacted the EP-3E's left outboard propeller just forward of the F-8 II's vertical stabilizer. The resulting structural damage caused the F-8 II to break in half and lose controlled flight. At the time of the collision, the EP-3E was flying on autopilot, straight and level. Debris from the PRC fighter impact destroyed the EP-3E's nose cone and damaged the number 1 and number 3 propellers and the number 1 engine. This damage caused the EP-3E to roll left nearly inverted and descend uncontrolled more than 8000 feet before the pilot recovered partial control.

Unable to maintain altitude or cabin pressurization, the EP-3E continued to descend another 6000 feet before full control was regained. The collision of the two aircraft occurred near position 1735N 11055E, approximately 70 nm southeast of Hainan Island

32 "The nature of the damage to the number 1 engine and the unknown extent of damage to the rest of the aircraft dictated that a landing take place as soon as possible, before the aircraft's condition further deteriorated. The navigator directed a course to Lingshui Airfield, where the pilot made a successful no-flap landing at 0134Z. No crew was injured during the incident. At 0141Z, the mission aircraft reported, 'On deck at Lingshui,' via secure satellite communications."

33 "Intelligence is the ability to adapt to change." - Stephen Hawking

34 "The greatest potential for PRC intelligence gains is in the area of analyzing and potentially emulating U.S. COMINT signals analysis equipment and methodology, especially the LUNCHBOX PROFORMA processor and MARTES analysis tools."

35 "(C) All data and software on both the SCARAB computer containing the LUNCHBOX PROFORMA processor and the laptop containing MARTES signals analysis tools were compromised."

36 "(S) PROFORMA signals are digital command and control data communications that relay information and instructions to and from radar systems, weapon systems (e.g., surface-to-air missiles, anti-aircraft artillery, fighter aircraft), and control centers. Exploitation of this information provides U.S. and allied warfighters nearly instantaneous situational awareness data from a target country's radar systems. This information supplements U.S. sensor systems while providing insight into the target country's decision process."

37 "The MARTES laptop also included a Radio Signals Notation (RASIN) Manual, RASIN Working Aid, and associated materials. Together, the RASIN manual and the aforementioned files provided a comprehensive overview of how the U.S. Cryptologic System exploits an adversary's signal environment."

38 "(S//SI) The PRC's most effective denial methods would be to move from current over-the-air transmissions to landline transmissions, or to more advanced radio communications techniques, such as frequency hopping, that could complicate the U.S. Cryptologic System's exploitation efforts. The PRC could also potentially deny future access by encrypting these signals, although encryption is not likely. PROFORMA signals are not routinely encrypted because of their perishable nature and the requirement to provide fast, dependable data throughput. However, some PROFORMA signals are"

39 "The overall damage from compromised information on the MARTES laptop is considered medium. The MARTES laptop sustained no visible damage (Figure 3), but its recovered hard drives were found to be shattered. Technical experts assess that the crew did not cause this damage. Based on all available data, we believe that the PRC copied the laptop's hard drives and then destroyed them. All data resident on the MARTES laptop, including signal identification and processing software, working aids, and signal samples, is considered compromised."

40   "The most sensitive and damaging documentation compromised was contained in collection requirements hardcopy documents that detail U.S. tasking against PRC military datalink and microwave signals. The tasking data, containing information such as frequencies, data rates, dish sizes, and target communicants, outlined the U.S. capability to exploit digital signals."

41   "The U.S. ability to collect PRC submarine signal transmissions and make subsequent vessel correlations was compromised. This compromise could prompt the PRC to modify the signal that the U.S. exploits to make vessel correlations. Although its ability to exploit these signals is limited, NSA is confident that the U.S. Cryptologic System could recover from any changes to the signal content."

42   "The most revealing and potentially damaging JQR materials compromised were completed JQRs and study guides for the PRC Navy Operator and COMEVAL positions. These JQR materials detailed specific target information (e.g., frequencies, units of interest) and described U.S. reconnaissance operating areas, programs, and collection platforms."

43   "The primary impact of the compromise of ELINT documentation would be in improved PRC electronic warfare planning against the U.S. and Taiwan."

44   "The limited damage to this equipment can be circumvented by a competent reverse engineering effort. It is assessed that all ELINT hardware systems on the aircraft have been fully compromised."

45   "The technologies resident in compromised ELINT systems would not advance present PRC technical capabilities. PRC radar and ELINT technologies are advanced to the point that they are capable of employing all techniques used on the EP-3E. The primary impact of the compromise of these systems would be in the operational lessons the PRC learns about U.S. ELINT techniques and procedures. These lessons, if properly applied, could help the PRC counter U.S. collection efforts as well as improve its tactical ELINT collection."

46   "There existed a unifying cryptologic strategy for preventing information from falling into an adversary's possession. Such a strategy exists in Information Assurance (IA), where it is assumed that COMSEC equipments will be compromised. The triad of controlled equipment, encrypted communications, and robust key management significantly mitigates the damage incurred through the loss or compromise of any single COMSEC element (see section 5.2). Conversely, SIGINT is founded on a 'no compromise' principle. SIGINT is to be protected at all times and, if it is deemed to be in jeopardy of compromise or loss, destroyed. This approach lacks flexibility and reflects an era when SIGINT capabilities resided on hardware and in hardcopy versus today's world where increasingly these capabilities reside in software."

48   "The greatest potential for PRC COMSEC gains is in the area of analyzing and potentially emulating U.S. COMSEC tradecraft."

49   "The EP-3E carried the complete complement of COMSEC equipments and keying materials necessary to conduct its SRO mission, including several KY-58 secure voice and KG-84 secure data devices (Figure 5),

KYK-13 and KOI-18 electronic fill devices, a KL-43 off-line encryption device, and a Global Positioning System (GPS) unit. The EP-3E also carried keying and other cryptographic materials for its various secure devices (see Appendix B for a complete list of equipments and cryptographic material onboard). Top Secret keying material in canisters, entire codebooks, and call sign lists were onboard. In all, the EP-3E carried COMSEC materials in excess of what was needed for the mission. Nearly a month's worth of keying material and codebook pages were carried that were not scheduled to become effective until well after the scheduled landing. COMSEC devices onboard included unused electronic fill devices and several installed spare encryption devices."

50 "Before departing the aircraft, the crew hand tore the paper materials and spread them throughout the aircraft. However, since the paper materials were not destroyed with approved equipment such as a crosscut shredder, the PRC would probably be able to reconstruct the key tape. U.S. experts have demonstrated the ability to reconstruct tape from pieces torn as the crew described. Examination of the recovered EP-3E revealed that some torn keying material was retained by the PRC."

51 "Compromised cryptographic materials might enable PRC SIGINT units to decrypt limited U.S. Pacific area encrypted transmissions for 31 March and 1 April. Since the PRC possessed the crypto-device from the EP-3E, they would have been able to decrypt communications if they had:

☒ Recorded and retained the communications for future exploitation, and

☒ Located and reconstructed the keying material that was hand torn and left onboard the aircraft."

52 "If PRC technicians successfully exploit the compromised EP-3E cryptographic material and devices, they would gain information as to how the U.S. incorporates these security designs. This insight could provide the PRC with an impetus to incorporate similar designs in its indigenous cryptographic materials and devices, making U.S. decryption efforts more difficult."

54 "(C) The overall potential foreign relations impact from compromise of materials onboard the EP-3E is assessed to be low."

55 "The compromised ELINT Parameters List included detailed emitter parameters for many radars and weapons systems of foreign partners."

56 "Compromised information included data acknowledging U.S. cryptologic relationships with Taiwan, Japan, South Korea, and Thailand; SOI related to the airspace of some partners, such as Taiwan; and PROFORMA data from some partner countries. This information was located onboard the EP-3E in software tools and hardcopy notes used by the cryptologic technicians. Information such as SOI enabled the aircraft to transit safely to its area of responsibility, conduct its mission, and return safely to its staging base. Other information was used to exploit communications of the PRC and several neighboring countries."

57 "The potential impact from PRC disclosure of the LUNCHBOX data to other countries is a concern. From a SIGINT perspective, the PRC's exploitation of LUNCHBOX and the disclosure of its PROFORMA capabilities to foreign partners could result in a loss of access to some foreign PROFORMA signals by the U.S. and its allies (see section 4.2).

From a foreign relations perspective, the fact that the U.S. has the ability to monitor the command and control environment of friendly and unfriendly nations would be of minor concern to some countries. NSA has developed notification procedures and will coordinate notification of foreign partners with appropriate Intelligence Community partners."

58 "The EP-3E incident was not the first compromise of U.S. tactical cryptologic sources and methods or other sensitive information to the PRC or its closest partners. North Korea's seizure of the USS Pueblo in 1968 and espionage cases in the 1980s and 1990s provided the PRC with insight into the U.S. Cryptologic System's targeting of its tactical and encrypted communications. There are indications that PRC operatives have actively sought to acquire U.S. COMSEC equipments and manuals. Additionally, one of the PRC's closest partners, Russia, has acquired similar information on U.S. targeting of special submarine communications, PROFORMA, and many of the USSIDs that were onboard the EP-3E. Although there is no direct evidence that Russia has shared any of this information with the PRC, the PRC has probably benefited from information gleaned from previously compromised equipment."

59 "Names and organizations of Intelligence Community and foreign partner personnel were disclosed in documentation onboard the EP-3E."

60 "In other cases, the PRC's efforts to reverse engineer some computer boards and chips were detectable only with a microscope."

61 "There have been no indications of any PRC recovery efforts other than initial search and recovery attempts focusing on the F-8 II and its pilot. The Office of Naval Intelligence is monitoring the area for signs of recovery activity, but limited U.S. collection assets in the region mean that it is possible that the PRC could conduct such a search without being detected."

62 "The EP-3E incident was multifaceted (e.g., military operational, diplomatic, intelligence compromise) but data flow beyond the normal military audience was initially limited."

63 "(S//SI) NSA's ability to know at any specific time the totality of overall collection against a specific target is fragmented. In a crisis response situation, the result is that typically 24 hours or more can pass before there is an accurate accounting of all national and tactical systems arrayed against a target. Although NSA immediately began to augment or "surge" collection by working with the Intelligence Community to steer systems such as overhead satellites to increase coverage of the PRC, other collection assets were not tasked as rapidly. Such a delay can result in important collection opportunities being forfeited in the early, and perhaps most important, stages of a crisis."

64 "NSA's National Security Operations Center (NSOC) served as the central clearinghouse for all EP-3E information with the Senior Operations Officer (SOO) handling requests from Defense, CIA, State, and White House officials. After two days, however, the deluge of calls began to impact the SOO's other duties. This led to a decision to establish an EP-3 desk to serve as the focal point for all EP-3E related matters. The EP-3 desk stood up officially on Tuesday, 3 April. Most customers praised NSOC's responsiveness and its twice-daily SIGINT updates.

Although the EP-3 desk performed well, customer inquiries eventually consumed most of the desk officers' time. Some customers sought an EP-3 website where they could go for related data, but such a site was not established during this crisis. Crisis-related websites at JICPAC and KRSOC were praised for their usefulness. In general, the operating forces and

65 "The EP-3E incident highlighted misunderstandings within the U.S. Cryptologic System regarding providing raw SIGINT to customers. For example, some managers had a false impression that the requests for raw SIGINT required legal review when in fact it is a policy, not a legal issue. Also, NSA officers in the field differed in their interpretations of their responsibilities to handle raw SIGINT."

66 "In order to increase the accuracy of future damage assessments, the intelligence debriefing process must be allowed sufficient time and be completed as soon as possible after such a compromise."

67 "(U//FOUO) The Secretary of Defense in coordination with the DCI should charter a damage assessment team within 48 hours of a potential intelligence compromise involving DoD assets. The team should serve as the lead for producing findings, the damage assessment, and recommendations."

68 "There was no policy guidance regarding actions to be taken in the event of hazardous maneuvers by reacting PRC fighter aircraft."

69 "The U.S. government was aware of the potential hazards imposed by such activity and delivered a demarche on the topic to Beijing in December 2000. However, neither the Pacific Command nor the JCS issued any new guidance regarding actions to be taken in the event of close encounters by reacting PRC fighter aircraft."

70 "(C) The flight crew defaulted to U.S. military emergency communications procedures that were ineffective in establishing contact with the PRC."

71 "The navigator transmitted MAYDAY calls on PTN. At least one transmission was received by both KRSOC and SSA, initiating CRITIC reporting. The navigator also transmitted MAYDAY calls on the GHFS frequency of 13200 kHz. These calls were never received."

72 "The inability to effectively communicate orders and intentions contributed significantly to the incomplete destruction effort."

73 "After the collision, the first command issued by the Mission Commander was to prepare to bail out. This command was issued via the PA. All crew members removed their headsets in order to don their parachutes, survival vests and helmets. High noise levels resulting from aircraft damage gave crew members wearing helmets great difficulty hearing each other, even when shouting at close range. PA announcements were also difficult to hear. At this point, communication of orders and instructions to the crew became unreliable."

74 "Others had taken assigned ditching stations in the galley, and had no DCMS access. As a result, many crew members did not realize the aircraft was landing instead of ditching until they either saw land out a window or heard the landing gear deploy."

75 "The aircrew did not limit classified material to that necessary for the conduct of the mission. Technical working aids contained material

covering Russia, North Korea, India, and the Persian Gulf, as well as intelligence on the PRC not relevant to the mission. Additionally, the crew carried substantial training materials and study aids not required for the mission."

76 "Ensure the Mission Commander and other personnel responsible for emergency destruction are fully cognizant of the scope and nature of all classified materials onboard the aircraft and are in compliance with USSID 3."

77 "There is no unifying concept underlying any of the guidance regarding emergency destruction."

78 "The aircraft's fire axe, a dull hatchet approximately 16 inches long intended for cutting through bulkheads in an emergency evacuation, was used in destruction attempts."

79 "The aircraft's fire axe was aggressively employed in attempts to destroy the three ELINT laptop computers. This technique is estimated to have been effective in destroying the hard drive of one laptop, but the other two laptop hard drives are assessed to have survived destruction attempts due in part to operator unfamiliarity with how best to destroy them."

80 "Individual crew performance during the emergency destruction activities ranged from good to poor. Effective communication among three key officers (the Mission Commander, SEVAL and COMEVAL) after the collision would have improved the outcome of emergency destruction. A lack of cohesive and unified crew training adversely affected emergency destruction."

81 "The aircrew's overall performance in safeguarding classified materials under their charge was poor. Success where it occurred was the result of the common sense focus of a few individuals in an uncoordinated effort and occurred despite a general lack of training, practice in emergency destruction, capabilities, and sound policy."

82 "There was a common view that the coordination and effortlessness that marks outstanding crews is difficult to achieve since training and preparation for the deployment occur separately, the responsibility of two different commands. Frequently, the entire crew for the mission aircraft does not meet as a unit until the first mission of the deployment."

83 "Assuming the destruction plans are technically appropriate for the materials onboard, crew training and drilling will be the deciding factor in successful emergency destruction."

84 "It is clear that a better-aligned and trained crew could have substantially mitigated, and likely completely avoided, the loss of sensitive material through better communication and more effective action."

85 "The U.S. requires a response that changes the paradigm from destruction of equipments and materials to safeguarding information with modern techniques such as encryption and rapid overwriting of hard disks. While destruction may always be preferred, it may not always be possible. Several Intelligence Community organizations are currently working on such applications and have deployed these capabilities on a limited scale. These efforts should be crosswalked, melded into a coherent program, and migrated into operational platforms and missions. This is imperative given that more classified and sensitive capability, not less, will find its way into

	risky environments where compromise is possible and where destruction is impractical or not possible."
86	"(U//FOUO) A report of critical information concerning possible foreign threats to U.S. national security that is so significant that it requires the immediate attention of the President and the National Security Council. CRITICs are delivered within 10 minutes to appropriate intelligence organizations, military components, and other recipients as the DCI may designate."
87	"(U) Technical and intelligence information obtained from the intercept and analysis of non-communication, electromagnetic radiations."
88	"(U) A small device that provides secure voice digital communications with FM, AM, VHF, and UHF radios. Designed for mounting in an aircraft instrument panel or radio console."
89	"Term Expansion Definition/Description PTN Pacific Tributary Network (U//FOUO) A dedicated UHF Satellite communications net providing 24-hour voice communications support between national and Pacific theater commands."
90	"ZIRCON Chat is a commercial internet relay chat application used on the secure Joint Worldwide Intelligence Communications System network. Allows multiple intelligence providers to communicate with deployed threat warning recipients."
91	"Recommendation #1 (U//FOUO) Limit classified and sensitive materials carried onboard SRO platforms to mission-essential materials only. Minimize hardcopy materials in favor of electronic media."
92	"Develop and implement configuration controls to govern the use of NSA-deployed software versions and maintain cognizance of field modifications; include procedures to annually overwrite all software with the most currently available software."
93	"Recommendation #22 (U//FOUO) The Secretary of Defense in coordination with the DCI should charter a damage assessment team within 48 hours of a potential compromise involving DoD assets. The team should serve as the lead for producing findings, damage assessment, and recommendations."
94	"Design and implement improved emergency communications procedures and hardware on the EP-3E to enable reliable communications at all times, especially during abnormal flight conditions. Investigate wireless communications systems."
95	"Issue policy to increase the detail in material inventories to support a rapid and accurate page-for-page reconstruction of all sensitive and classified materials, including all files on hard disks, CD ROMs, and floppy disks."
96	"Recommendation #62 (U//FOUO) Implement, track, and institutionalize the study's recommendations."
97	"The following USSID material was determined to compromised either entirely or partially. Most of the hardcopy USSID material was not carried onboard in its entirety, but was mentioned or partially described in Job Qualification Requirements (JQR), Working Aids, and personal notes. The following material was not destroyed and was left onboard the aircraft in a storage locker."

98	"Combining what we know about these efforts, expert testimony, and analysis of the returned laptop, there is a very low likelihood that sensitive cryptologic information could be recovered. As a result, all USSID material listed below is considered as a possible compromise."
99	"Hardcopy and softcopy COMINT material was carried onboard the aircraft. The hardcopy material listed below was intact or hand-shredded and left onboard the EP-3E. All material is considered to be compromised."
100	"Map of Spratly Islands"
101	"Integrated Air Defense System (IADS) - Handwritten notes"
104	"PRC Aircraft including indicators - Activity (local airfield, basic flight, combat training, reactions, live intercept, defensive patrols, navigation training and inter-airfield flights, bomber activity) - Transcription requirements"
105	"NKAF Air Order of Battle - NKAF Fighter/Bomber characteristics - SAM indications and sites - Map of NKAF significant placenames - Hand-written notes in JQR - USSID identification - Radio/telephone procedures - U.S. Fleet organization - Command/MCOC organization - Warfighter Communications paths (TRE, TRAP, TDDS, TOPS, TIBS) - COMINT releasability caveats (SEABOOT, SETTEE, KAMPUS, DRUID, RORIPA, NOFORN, ORCON) - Callsign definitions - NK Air Defense System - NK SAM force - UNACCENTED description (not in detail) - NK MRBM Launch indicators - NK Reacting Airfields - NK Infiltration Operations - PRC Airfields and aircraft locations - PRC Reacting Airfields - PRC Naval Auxiliary vessel classes - PRC ASV Tracking Stations - Russian PACOFAF, PVO/TAF, and SAF Airfields -
106	"(S//SI) The COMINT Supervisor's laptop contained softcopy COMINT material (as well as USSID material detailed previously). The material listed below is considered as a possible compromise, given our assessment that there is a very low likelihood of recovering data from the laptop."
107	"The list of materials below was left onboard the EP-3E, either intact or hand-shredded, and is considered compromised."
108	"Russian Far East Military District (FEMD) Air Order of Battle - Association of fighter and bomber aircraft with airfields - Standard aircraft weapon and radar fits - Association of ELNOTs with NATO names and standard parametric bands of radars"
109	"The ELINT Evaluator's laptop computer was destroyed by the crew and left onboard the aircraft. The laptop hard drive was recovered, though not found with the laptop. Both were analyzed by NSA experts and it was determined that the hard drive probably survived crew destruction attempts only to be copied and then destroyed by the PRC. All data resident on this system is considered compromised."
110	"The bulk of the ELINT systems are off-the-shelf devices that, although designed for the ELINT mission, contain no particularly sensitive technologies. Two systems that represent a specific concern include the AN/ULQ-16 and the AN/ALQ-108."
111	"The recovery team determined that the equipment was at a minimum examined by the PRC. There were signs of PRC intrusion into many

pieces of equipment that could indicate PRC attempts at reverse engineering."

112 "The EP-3 Assessment Team requested that NSA's Office of Foreign Relations provide information on the impact of the EP-3E compromise to NSA's cryptologic foreign partners. This appendix provides NSA's response and identifies internal actions that NSA will take to notify foreign partners."

113 "The Office of Foreign Relations recommends no action be initiated with foreign governments. If leaked, the Office of Foreign Relations recommends in general that a position of not commenting on the details of US intelligence activities be maintained, but reserves the right to respond on a case-by-case basis to certain partner nations."

114 "We do not believe the Thai partner SIGINT agency or government should be advised of the compromise, because of the newness of the current partner leadership and the tenuous political situation in Thailand."

115 "Fact of geographic areas of DSD, GCHQ, and CSE TEXTA authority; Compromise of GCHQ RASIN Manual Working Aid; CSE Telegraphic Codes Manual; DSD document on AN/ULQ-16 Operations at Kangaroo 95 (ADF exercise)."

116 "The SCARAB will never be powered up during the test sequence."

117 "There are two basic tests that will be performed on one of the laptops. The second laptop will be held in spare as well as used to verify the operation of the disks after they have been tested and analyzed for the purposes of recovery."

118 "(C) Generally, results from the re-created destruction tests revealed the difficulty of disabling a computer system with shock by dropping, stomping, or striking the equipment. For each of the three systems tested, results did not damage the computers enough to conclude that data recovery was impossible. This underscores the importance of providing clear instructions and training for how to physically destroy computers."

119 "The Global High Frequency System (GHFS) is a worldwide network of high-power HF stations that provides air/ground HF command and control radio communications between ground agencies and U.S. military aircraft. The GHFS network supports SRO aircraft by passing encoded NICKELBACK advisory conditions, position reports and administrative traffic."

120 "The Pacific Tributary Network (PTN) is a UHF secure voice satellite network that provides COMINT advisory support and threat warning to U.S. and allied forces in the theater."

122 "The visits focused on gaining insights into best practices for risk mitigation in the day-to-day conduct of tactical intelligence, surveillance and reconnaissance (ISR) missions."

123 "Emergency Destruction is ordered by the pilot (aircraft commander), lead electronic warfare officer (tactical controller (TC)), or airborne mission supervisor (AMS). Once destruction is initiated, aircrew members use their position checklists, which identify their respective responsibilities."

124 "In an emergency situation, the DSO zeroizes all crypto devices, clears his laptop computers, destroys the hard drives of both laptops using a 9MM handgun or an axe, and adds water to the water soluble papers of the technical working aid."

125 "If enemy attack is imminent, then all classified equipment, to include the vehicle would be destroyed using thermite grenades."

127 "White House NSC Intel Director, Deputy Director, Situation Room, CIA DDCI MA, Lt Gen ADCI Collection, D/ADCI Anal & Prod, Congress, SSCI, HPSCI, HPSCI HPSCI"

129 "The collision incident requires a comprehensive, fully coordinated, end-to-end damage assessment, including a review of emergency procedures and actions, development of lessons learned, and recommendations for corrective action, where appropriate."

131 "The final report, with an Executive Summary and briefing, will be delivered to the CNO and DIRNSA. It will include a:
- Summary of the incident from collision to repatriation
- Damage assessment of SIGINT and IA equipment, techniques, and information compromised
- Review and assessment of operational activities
- Counterintelligence assessment
- Review of SIGINT and IA crisis response
- Consolidated lessons learned and near-, mid-, and long-term recommendations, including action agencies and deliverable timelines"

132 "Team/group composition must balanced in size and expertise.
- Information must be managed to avoid premature disclosure and to protect the fact finding process.
- 'Protected' lists of authorized recipients will be created to guide dissemination for each team and overall assessment. Release of information beyond the list of authorized recipients will be controlled by CNO and DIRNSA. Follow-on information requirements for the EP-3E crew can be anticipated."

TOP SECRET//COMINT//NOFORN//X1

EP-3E Collision:
Cryptologic Damage Assessment and Incident Review

Final Report

Prepared by the
EP-3 Cryptologic Assessment Team
July 2001

Classified by: NSA/CSS Classification Manual
　　　　Dated: 23 February 1998
Declassify on: X1　　　　　　　　　　　　　　　　　　　　　Copy # _____

TOP SECRET//COMINT//NOFORN//X1

TOP SECRET//COMINT//NOFORN//X1

(U) Preface

(U//FOUO) On 1 April 2001, a People's Republic of China (PRC) F-8-II fighter collided with a U.S. Navy EP-3E electronic surveillance aircraft operating over the South China Sea. The EP-3E aircraft survived the collision and subsequently recovered in the PRC at Lingshui Airfield on Hainan Island. The crew was detained by the PRC for 11 days before being repatriated to the United States. This report is a review and assessment of the EP-3E incident, as directed by the Chief of Naval Operations (CNO) and the Director, National Security Agency/Chief, Central Security Service (DIRNSA).

(U//FOUO) The information used to prepare this report was derived from two rounds of debriefing the 24 EP-3E crew members, a review of documentation relevant to the conduct of airborne SIGINT surveillance operations, interviews with numerous individuals and organizations associated with the event, data collected from reenacted destruction testing, and analysis of the recovered aircraft. This report details the materials and equipments presumed compromised to the PRC and estimates the damage from the compromise. It describes the crew's reactions from the time of the collision until the crew and aircraft came under control of the PRC at Lingshui Airfield. It reviews emergency processes and procedures, potential PRC actions, foreign relations impact, counterintelligence issues, and cryptologic crisis response. Finally, the report recommends actions to minimize and manage the risk of like events in the future.

(U//FOUO) This is a final report, delivered to the CNO and DIRNSA. All previous reports of cryptologic loss and impact from this event are superseded. The Commander, Naval Security Group, is responsible for coordinating analysis and reporting of any subsequent findings developed from examination of the recovered EP-3E.

TOP SECRET//COMINT//NOFORN//X1

TOP SECRET//COMINT//NOFORN//X1

(U) Executive Summary

(S) The collision of a PRC F-8-II with a U.S. EP-3E over the South China Sea on 1 April 2001 triggered a series of events, the outcomes of which ranged from very good to very poor. Through superb airmanship and teamwork, 24 crew members and an $80 million aircraft were saved. COMSEC keying material and ELINT data were largely jettisoned. The crew acquitted themselves well while detained. Conversely, sensitive COMINT equipment, large volumes of technical data, and SIGINT policy directives were compromised.

(S) This assessment addresses two interrelated tasks. The first was to review and assess the damage to cryptologic sources and methods from the compromise of COMSEC and SIGINT material and the response of the U.S. Cryptologic System (USCS) to the crisis. The second was to review and assess emergency destruction, classified material handling, communications, and emergency procedures.

(S) The USCS response to the crisis was generally good. The report makes some recommendations regarding policy and dissemination that should further improve customer support. NSA's separate internal look at its crisis procedures promises to result in additional improvements.

(S) Damage to U.S. COMSEC products and methods, i.e., cryptographic devices, keying material, and encryption methodology, was low, primarily due to design philosophy. Cryptographic devices are designed in anticipation of being lost or compromised. The significant portion of the encryption process –the key– is normally changed daily. Without the key, adversaries cannot decrypt or read U.S. communications, even if they have obtained the cryptographic device and have the target communications. Procedures for superseding key are routine and efficient. In this incident, within 15 hours of the EP-3E's landing in the PRC, all keying materials, except for the Global Positioning System (GPS) worldwide key, were superseded. The crew jettisoned most of the onboard keying material.

(S) There is no such holistic approach for SIGINT material. The assumption has been that sensitive SIGINT material will be protected or destroyed before it is lost or compromised. However, events again proved this premise wrong. Emergency destruction techniques have not kept pace with technology and are not always suited for an era where capabilities reside in software, not hardware. When, for a variety of reasons, emergency destruction was not carried out effectively, compromise of SIGINT capabilities to the PRC resulted. Damage to the whole of U.S. and allied SIGINT capability against the PRC is assessed to be low (i.e., little or no damage, recoverable in the normal course of operations). Damage in the realm of tactical SIGINT is assessed to be medium (i.e., significant damage, recoverable with concerted effort). These are worst-case assessments. Importantly, no national sources or methods were compromised.

TOP SECRET//COMINT//NOFORN//X1

TOP SECRET//COMINT//NOFORN//X1

(S) The EP-3E incident revealed SIGINT emergency destruction procedures to be outdated and inadequate. Moreover, individual and crew training were deficient. Emergency destruction training –when practiced– lacked realism and context. There were no readily available means or standard procedures for timely destruction of computers, electronic media, and hardcopy material. Procedures for control of classified information were generally adequate but not followed completely. Configuration of SIGINT systems and software lacked policy standards and management guidelines. Finally, destruction activities were complicated by communication problems. The crew's ability to communicate was impacted by noise, system configuration, and the kaleidoscope of actions attendant to preparations for bailing out, then ditching, and finally, landing at Lingshui. Notwithstanding the chaotic circumstances on the aircraft following the collision, we conclude that the crew had sufficient time to jettison all sensitive materials. We believe that better policy, training, communications, and capabilities would have improved the outcome of the emergency destruction efforts.

(S) Prompt corrective action is needed in many areas. Foremost is a need to address a systemic complacency regarding the safeguarding of sensitive information. This incident clearly demonstrates the power of the unitary approach taken for COMSEC material, one founded on the assumption that material will be lost or compromised and that safeguarding information, not destroying material, is the ultimate goal. This philosophy led to creation of a regime designed to prevent exploitation of U.S. communications despite loss or compromise. A similar approach to SIGINT systems and information is needed commencing with the same goal of safeguarding information by preventing exploitation. From that basis, it is possible to shape specific means (e.g., physical destruction, encryption, overwriting data) with governing standards, configuration management, and training to reduce or even eliminate damage from loss or compromise of SIGINT information.

(S) In the course of our inquiries, many have suggested the need for a universal solution to SIGINT destruction. Because of the range of current capabilities in use, we have not found one. New safeguard capabilities are needed. Promising areas of development include the use of encryption techniques to render information on a laptop useless if compromised. As plans call for more and increasingly sensitive SIGINT capabilities to be fielded, new safeguard capabilities are required not only for SRO platforms, but for all SIGINT collection activities at risk.

(U//FOUO) This report makes recommendations for improvements and suggests an action agency for each. Some are already completed or ongoing. All need to be tracked to completion, examined for applicability across all activities, not just SRO, and institutionalized. Failure to address these issues decisively will not just continue the likelihood of future losses, it will guarantee it.

TOP SECRET//COMINT//NOFORN//X1

(U) Key Findings

(U//FOUO) The EP-3 Cryptologic Assessment Team reached the following conclusions:

- (S) Potential damage to tactical U.S. SIGINT capabilities against the PRC from the compromise of tactical sources and methods is assessed to be medium.
- (S) Potential damage to overall U.S. SIGINT capabilities against the PRC as a result of materials compromised is assessed to be low.
- (S//SI) The greatest potential for PRC intelligence gains is in the area of analyzing and potentially emulating U.S. COMINT signals analysis equipment and methodology, especially the LUNCHBOX PROFORMA processor and MARTES analysis tools.
- (U//FOUO) The incident revealed a systemic complacency regarding policy, planning, and training support to EP-3E SRO missions.
- (S) Overall damage resulting from the compromise of cryptographic equipments and materials is assessed to be low.
- (S) The greatest potential for PRC COMSEC gains is in the area of analyzing and potentially emulating U.S. COMSEC tradecraft.
- (S//SI) The fact of the U.S. ability to acquire and locate signals associated with PRC submarines was compromised.
- (S//SI) National-level U.S. SIGINT (e.g., Special Collection Service, Overhead, Clandestine SIGINT) sources and methods were not compromised.
- (S//SI) As of July 2001, the U.S. Cryptologic System has not detected any changes to PRC or other countries' communications resulting from the EP-3E compromise.
- (S//SI) Compromised signals processing capabilities will not allow the PRC to make any advances in exploiting U.S. encryption systems, nor will it allow the PRC to discover any flaws in the protection of its own communications.
- (U//FOUO) There was no configuration management process in place for control and inventory of deployed SIGINT materials and equipments.
- (C) The overall potential foreign relations impact from compromise of materials onboard the EP-3E is assessed to be low.
- (C) The EP-3E incident was multifaceted (e.g., military operational, diplomatic, intelligence compromise) but data flow beyond the normal military audience was initially limited.
- (C) Restrictions on dissemination of "raw" SIGINT led to frustration and misunderstanding among some customers.
- (U//FOUO) No specific guidance existed regarding Mission Commander or aircrew actions should an SRO aircraft be forced or, through emergency, be required to land in the PRC.
- (C) A substantial amount of non-mission-essential classified information was carried onboard the aircraft.

TOP SECRET//COMINT//NOFORN//X1

TOP SECRET//COMINT//NOFORN//X1

- (C) Inventory procedures did not require sufficient detail to identify reliably the content of classified equipments, computers, or hardcopy materials.
- (C) Crew training for emergency destruction was minimal and did not meet squadron requirements; this deficiency was the primary cause of the compromise of classified material.
- (C) There was sufficient time to jettison all sensitive materials from the aircraft.

TOP SECRET//COMINT//NOFORN//X1

(U) Table of Contents

(U) **Preface**		iii
(U) **Executive Summary**		v
(U) **Key Findings**		vii
1.0	(U) **Introduction**	1
2.0	(U) **Methodology**	3
3.0	(U) **Collision Incident Summary**	5
4.0	(U) **SIGINT Review and Assessment**	9

    4.1   (U) Key Findings
    4.2   (U) COMINT Equipment and Documentation
    4.3   (U) ELINT Equipment and Documentation
    4.4   (U) SIGINT Configuration and Materials Management

5.0	(U) **IA Review and Assessment**	23

    5.1   (U) Key Findings
    5.2   (U) Cryptographic Tutorial
    5.3   (U) Cryptographic Materials and Equipments
    5.4   (C) Potential for PRC Intelligence Gain from IA Compromises

6.0	(U) **PRC Potential Actions and the Cryptologic Response**	29

    6.1   (U) Key Finding
    6.2   (U) SIGINT Collection Strategy
    6.3   (U) Cryptologic Foreign Partner Impact
    6.4   (U) PRC Sharing and Previous Access to Compromised Data
    6.5   (U) Counterintelligence Issues
    6.6   (C) Potential for Recovery of Jettisoned Equipment

7.0	(U) **U.S. Cryptologic System Crisis Response**	37

    7.1   (U) Key Findings
    7.2   (U) SIGINT Support
    7.3   (U) IA Crisis Response
    7.4   (U) Crisis Management
    7.5   (U) Communications and Interagency Coordination
    7.6   (U) SIGINT Policy Issues
    7.7   (U) Customer Views

TOP SECRET//COMINT//NOFORN//X1

TOP SECRET//COMINT//NOFORN//X1

    7.8   (U) Crew Debriefing Procedures
    7.9   (U) Damage Assessment Procedures
    7.10 (U) Recommendations

8.0   (U) Emergency Processes and Procedures   43

    8.1   (U) Key Findings
    8.2   (U) Policy
    8.3   (U) Radio Communications
    8.4   (U) Internal Communications
    8.5   (U) Classified and Sensitive Material Handling
    8.6   (U) Emergency Destruction Policy, Procedures, and Training
    8.7   (U) Crew Reaction
    8.8   (U) Other Tactical SIGINT Platforms

9.0   (U) Systemic Issues   59

    9.1   (U) Key Finding
    9.2   (U) Discussion
    9.3   (U) Recommendation

(U) Glossary   61

(U) Appendices

Appendix A	(U) Summary of Recommendations	66
Appendix B	(U//FOUO) List of Cryptologic Equipment and Information Compromised	72
Appendix C	(U//FOUO) Cryptologic Foreign Partner Impact	87
Appendix D	(U) Destruction Test Procedures	91
Appendix E	(U) EP-3E Radio Equipment and Networks	94
Appendix F	(U) Schematic of EP-3E with Position Identifications	96
Appendix G	(U) Other Tactical SIGINT Platforms	97
Appendix H	(U) Crisis Response Interviews	101
Appendix I	(U//FOUO) EP-3 Cryptologic Assessment Team Members	103
Appendix J	(U//FOUO) EP-3 Incident Assessment and Review Terms of Reference	104

TOP SECRET//COMINT//NOFORN//X1

TOP SECRET//COMINT//NOFORN//X1

1.0 (U) Introduction

(C) The EP-3E incident resulted in compromise of classified and sensitive Signals Intelligence (SIGINT) and Communications Security (COMSEC) equipment and information. It also illuminated deficiencies in policy, emergency procedures, and classified material control.

(C) For damage assessment purposes, we have assumed the worst case, i.e., the PRC will fully exploit the compromised equipments and materials and apply what it learns to maximum advantage. It may be several years before we can judge how the PRC actually applies intelligence gained from the compromised information, and any such assessment will be conducted against the backdrop of ongoing upgrades to PRC capabilities. In some instances, we are highly confident of the nature and extent of data compromised; in other cases, such as those involving electronic media or the contents of personal notes and working aids, we are less confident. Factors affecting our confidence include the effectiveness of attempted destruction of the equipment, PRC ability to recover data from damaged media, the accuracy of crew member recall regarding classified information in their control, and configuration management practices.

(C) This assessment focuses on potential gains to the PRC from compromised equipments and materials. Damage could increase if the PRC shares compromised information with other nations.

(C) To characterize damage to SIGINT sources and methods and COMSEC products and methods, we use low, medium, and high ratings. Each term refers to the ability of the U.S. Cryptologic System to recover from the compromise:

- Low: Little or no damage, recoverable with a normal level of effort.
- Medium: Significant damage, recoverable with concerted effort.
- High: Grave damage, assessed to be unrecoverable.

TOP SECRET//COMINT//NOFORN//X1

2.0 (U) Methodology

(C) The Chief of Naval Operations (CNO) and the Director, National Security Agency (DIRNSA) established the EP-3 Cryptologic Assessment Team on 27 April 2001. The team's purpose was to assess the cryptologic damage from the EP-3E's landing on Hainan Island and to make recommendations to improve processes and procedures for future Sensitive Reconnaissance Operations (SRO) missions. Representatives from the Department of the Navy, National Security Agency, Department of the Air Force, and Department of the Army served as members of the team. The team focused on all materials and equipments onboard the EP-3E when it departed its staging base in Japan, actions and decision-making during the mission and until repatriation, and the condition of recovered cryptologic materials and equipments. To accomplish the assessment, the team reviewed all materials from the crew's Hawaii debriefs, re-interviewed the entire crew in Maryland, met with Intelligence Community personnel, examined an EP-3E at Patuxent Naval Air Station, visited units engaged in SRO missions, reenacted destruction testing, and analyzed the recovered aircraft.

(U//FOUO) To promote openness, Navy mishap procedures were followed. Thus, a confidentiality memorandum, authorized by the Secretary of the Navy, was offered to and accepted by each individual. This agreement stated that any information provided by the crew would be used only for the purposes of this damage assessment and would not be made available for any other purpose. The purpose for offering a promise of confidentiality was to overcome any reluctance of an individual to reveal complete and candid information surrounding the event.

(U//FOUO) The team received invaluable assistance from the Joint Personnel Recovery Agency (JPRA) which played a primary role in repatriating the crew. JPRA personnel provided unique insight on the Hawaii debriefings and trained assessment team members on interview techniques and processes. The JPRA psychologist who accompanied the crew in Hawaii was also present with the team and the crew throughout the Maryland re-interviews.

(C) Further examination of returned EP-3E systems and other carry-on materials may yield additional insight into the PRC's success in exploiting this compromise. The Commander, Naval Security Group, is responsible for coordinating analysis and reporting of any subsequent findings developed from examination of the recovered EP-3E. Also, continued vigilance by the Intelligence Community for signals, human, and imagery intelligence that might indicate that the PRC is using data gleaned from this compromise is prudent.

TOP SECRET//COMINT//NOFORN//X1

3.0 (U) Collision Incident Summary

(S//SI) At 1947Z on 31 March 2001, an EP-3E aircraft (Bureau Number 156511) departed Kadena Air Base, Okinawa, Japan, with 24 crew members onboard for a scheduled CINCPACFLT-tasked Sensitive Reconnaissance Operations (SRO) mission in the South China Sea. The crew's primary tasking was to monitor the signals environment of the People's Republic of China (PRC), with emphasis on PRC South Sea Fleet tactical communications, radars, and weapons systems.

(S//NF) The mission aircraft proceeded southwest from Okinawa to SRO track 5Q2002 (Figure 1), flying west between Taiwan and the Philippines before following the coastline of the PRC past Hong Kong toward Hainan Island. The mission aircraft then flew steadily in a southwesterly direction approximately 60 nautical miles (nm) off the coast of Hainan Island in international airspace. Activity was light, with only Early Warning and Air Traffic Control radars and routine military communications checks intercepted. The EP-3E was steady on course 220 at 22,500 feet, flying at an airspeed of 185 knots. Weather was clear with seven-mile visibility and a broken cloud layer at 15,000 feet.

(S//SI) Beginning at approximately 0043Z, Chinese linguists aboard the EP-3E and operators at the Kunia Regional Security Operations Center (KRSOC) intercepted activity on Lingshui Airfield's primary frequency. The activity included ground controller and pilot communications checks, fighter pre-flight activities, takeoff

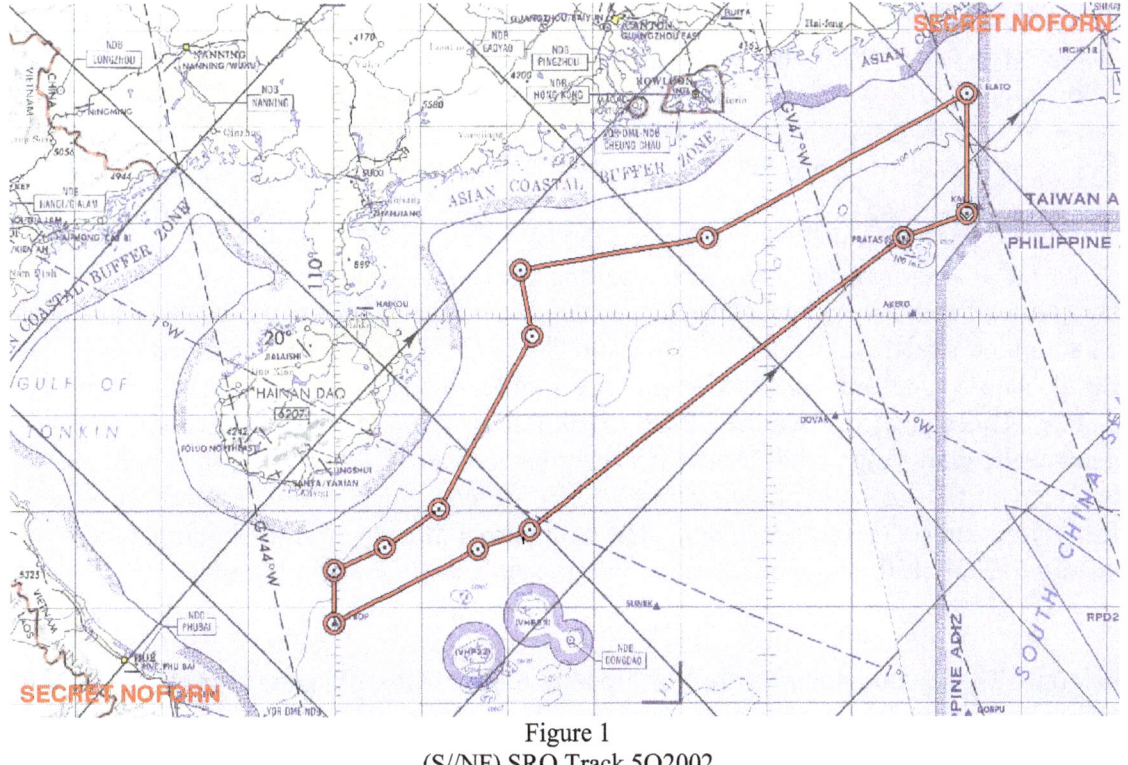

Figure 1
(S//NF) SRO Track 5Q2002

TOP SECRET//COMINT//NOFORN//X1

TOP SECRET//COMINT//NOFORN//X1

sequence, and ground-controlled intercept. At this time the EP-3E was approximately 70 nm due east of Lingshui near the end of its outbound leg and approaching its turnpoint to return to base. Between 0048Z-0049Z both the mission aircraft and KRSOC issued advisories on the PRC reaction to the presence of the EP-3E. At 0051Z, the mission aircraft acknowledged receipt of the KRSOC advisory via secure satellite communications.

(C) The EP-3E reported visual contact with two F-8 II fighters at 0055Z. The Mission Commander and Senior Evaluator decided to make the last turn to the northeast early, before the fighters moved closer to the EP-3E. The Mission Commander initiated a slow left turn, steadying on course 070 by 0100Z. During the turn, the PRC fighters maintained a distance of approximately one mile from the EP-3E.

(C) At approximately 0102Z, one fighter commenced the first of three distinct approaches to the mission aircraft from its left rear quarter while the other fighter maintained station approximately one half-mile behind, below, and to the left of the mission aircraft. On the first approach, the fighter closed to within ten feet of the mission aircraft. The PRC pilot rendered a salute and fell back to approximately 100 feet off the left wing of the EP-3E. At 0103Z, the same fighter approached the mission aircraft a second time, closing to within five feet. While in close formation with the mission aircraft, the PRC pilot was observed with his oxygen mask unfastened, gesturing to the EP-3E. The fighter then fell back to approximately 100 feet off the left wing.

(S//SI) At 0104Z, the PRC fighter closed on the mission aircraft again, exhibiting a much greater closure rate than in the previous two approaches. In an apparent maneuver to decrease his closure rate, the PRC pilot increased his angle of attack. Although the maneuver did decrease the closure rate, it placed the fighter directly below, and in very close proximity to, the EP-3E's left wing. At 0105Z, the PRC pilot reported that he was unable to maneuver and was being sucked in by the EP-3E.

(C) At 0105Z, the F-8 II impacted the EP-3E's left outboard propeller just forward of the F-8 II's vertical stabilizer. The resulting structural damage caused the F-8 II to break in half and lose controlled flight. At the time of the collision, the EP-3E was flying on autopilot, straight and level. Debris from the PRC fighter impact destroyed the EP-3E's nose cone and damaged the number 1 and number 3 propellers and the number 1 engine. This damage caused the EP-3E to roll left nearly inverted and descend uncontrolled more than 8000 feet before the pilot recovered partial control. Unable to maintain altitude or cabin pressurization, the EP-3E continued to descend another 6000 feet before full control was regained. The collision of the two aircraft occurred near position 1735N 11055E, approximately 70 nm southeast of Hainan Island.

(C) While still in the dive, the Mission Commander ordered the crew to prepare to bail out. Then, with partial control restored but the aircraft still losing altitude, the Mission Commander gave the order to prepare to ditch. At 0113Z, the aircraft issued a MAYDAY call via its secure satellite communications and indicated a mission abort, on course 300 degrees at 240 knots. Once the flight crew was able to maintain altitude at

TOP SECRET//COMINT//NOFORN//X1

TOP SECRET//COMINT//NOFORN//X1

8000 feet, they weighed their bail out and ditching options. Given the uncertainty of the crew's chance of surviving a bailout and the low likelihood of the damaged and difficult-to-control EP-3E surviving a ditching attempt, the Mission Commander elected to try to land the aircraft.

(C) The nature of the damage to the number 1 engine and the unknown extent of damage to the rest of the aircraft dictated that a landing take place as soon as possible, before the aircraft's condition further deteriorated. The navigator directed a course to Lingshui Airfield, where the pilot made a successful no-flap landing at 0134Z. No crew was injured during the incident. At 0141Z, the mission aircraft reported, "On deck at Lingshui," via secure satellite communications.

(C) Prior to landing, repeated EP-3E MAYDAY calls and requests for assistance on an international distress frequency (243.0 MHz) went unanswered by PRC controllers at Lingshui. Continuing attempts to contact the tower without success, the EP-3E conducted a clearing pass over the airfield at Lingshui before landing. Upon landing, the aircraft taxied under truck escort, parked off the edge of the runway and continued running engines for approximately ten minutes before shutting down. Approximately 20-24 PRC military personnel were in the vicinity of the EP-3E, six to eight of whom were armed with bolt-action weapons. The PRC military personnel did not point weapons at the aircrew, but the Mission Commander assessed that they were getting impatient. At approximately 0200Z, the Mission Commander ordered the crew to deplane, placing the crew and the aircraft in PRC control.

TOP SECRET//COMINT//NOFORN//X1

4.0 (U) SIGINT Review and Assessment

4.1 (U) Key Findings

- (S) Potential damage to tactical U.S. SIGINT capabilities against the PRC from the compromise of tactical sources and methods is assessed to be medium.
- (S) Potential damage to overall U.S. SIGINT capabilities against the PRC as a result of materials compromised is assessed to be low.
- (S//SI) The greatest potential for PRC intelligence gains is in the area of analyzing and potentially emulating U.S. COMINT signals analysis equipment and methodology, especially the LUNCHBOX PROFORMA processor and MARTES analysis tools.
- (S//SI) The fact of the U.S. ability to acquire and locate signals associated with PRC submarines was compromised.
- (S//SI) National-level U.S. SIGINT (e.g., Special Collection Service, Overhead, Clandestine SIGINT) sources and methods were not compromised.
- (S//SI) As of July 2001, the U.S. Cryptologic System has not detected any changes to PRC or other countries' communications resulting from the EP-3E compromise.
- (S//SI) Compromised signals processing capabilities will not allow the PRC to make any advances in exploiting U.S. encryption systems, nor will it allow the PRC to discover any flaws in the protection of its own communications.
- (U//FOUO) There was no configuration management process in place for control and inventory of deployed SIGINT materials and equipments.

4.1.1 (U) Introduction

(S//SI) The EP-3E carried a complete complement of SIGINT materials and equipments necessary to conduct its SRO mission against the PRC. In addition to installed equipment, six carry-on computers were onboard. The most potentially damaging compromised items were the carry-on LUNCHBOX PROFORMA processor and a laptop computer with MARTES software tools for collecting, analyzing, and processing signals. The aircraft also had an extensive inventory of SIGINT documentation in both hardcopy and electronic media. All SIGINT materials believed compromised are listed in Appendix B.

(S//SI) Damage to tactical U.S. SIGINT efforts against the PRC as a result of materials compromised is assessed to be medium. Tactical collection –those missions conducted by mobile collection platforms such as the EP-3E– represents only one facet of the overall cryptologic system sources and methods. Information on national-level U.S. SIGINT collection sources and methods, such as the Special Collection Service, Overhead, or Clandestine SIGINT, was not compromised. Additionally, SIGINT sources and methods of Second and Third Party foreign partner nations were not compromised. Overall damage, therefore, to U.S. SIGINT efforts against the PRC as a result of materials compromised is assessed to be low.

TOP SECRET//COMINT//NOFORN//X1

TOP SECRET//COMINT//NOFORN//X1

(S) This section reviews potential damage to the U.S. SIGINT system by first examining Communications Intelligence (COMINT), and then Electronic Intelligence (ELINT). Both equipment (e.g., carry-on computers, installed equipment) and documentation (e.g., technical data, working aids, crew notes) are discussed.

4.2 (U) COMINT Equipment and Documentation

(U//FOUO) This section focuses on COMINT, including PROFORMA. The two most sensitive systems onboard, LUNCHBOX and MARTES, are discussed in this section.

4.2.1 (U) Findings

- (C) All data and software on both the SCARAB computer containing the LUNCHBOX PROFORMA processor and the laptop containing MARTES signals analysis tools were compromised.
- (S) Overall, compromised PROFORMA-related material could provide the PRC with an understanding of U.S. PROFORMA exploitation capabilities.
- (S//SI) Compromised working aids and PROFORMA-related USSIDs provide detail about Russian-designed PROFORMA signals used in North Korea, Russia, Vietnam, and possibly the PRC.
- (S//SI) A tape containing enciphered and unenciphered PRC Navy communications was compromised.
- (S//SI) SIGINT technical information, such as Signals Operating Instructions (e.g., frequencies, call signs, and target identification data) and information from 23 USSIDs or excerpt of USSIDs were compromised.
- (S) Compromised COMINT documentation included collection tasking instructions, working aids, and notes focused on Far East Asian targets, as well as detailed crew member Job Qualification Requirements (JQR).
- (S//SI) The most sensitive documentation compromised was collection requirement tasking against specific PRC military datalink and microwave signals. This material provides insight into U.S. exploitation of these signals.
- (S//SI) Compromised tasking instructions revealed that the U.S. has acquired data on an advanced PRC communications system still under development.
- (S//SI) U.S. knowledge, at the SECRET//COMINT level, of the PRC Submarine Launched Ballistic Missile program was compromised.
- (S) Compromised SIGINT equipment and material may prompt the PRC to initiate or expedite COMSEC enhancements.

4.2.2 (U) COMINT Equipment

(U//FOUO) COMINT equipment onboard consisted of three carry-on computers (the SCARAB computer and two laptops) and installed COMINT equipment.

4.2.2.1 (U) LUNCHBOX PROFORMA Processor

TOP SECRET//COMINT//NOFORN//X1

TOP SECRET//COMINT//NOFORN//X1

(S) PROFORMA signals are digital command and control data communications that relay information and instructions to and from radar systems, weapon systems (e.g., surface-to-air missiles, anti-aircraft artillery, fighter aircraft), and control centers. Exploitation of this information provides U.S. and allied warfighters nearly instantaneous situational awareness data from a target country's radar systems. This information supplements U.S. sensor systems while providing insight into the target country's decision process.

(S//SI) For this particular mission, the Science and Technology (S&T) Operator was tasked to collect and process PROFORMA signals possibly associated with PRC SA-10 surface-to-air missiles and PRC short-range air navigation. The SCARAB portable computer loaded with the LUNCHBOX PROFORMA processor (Figure 2) was used for this task. The LUNCHBOX processor provides unique capabilities to process worldwide PROFORMA signals and contains electronic media documentation pertaining to many of those signals.

Figure 2
(C) Recovered LUNCHBOX PROFORMA processor

(S//SI) The LUNCHBOX processor's capabilities are substantial. Its software can process 40 worldwide PROFORMA signals; some teleprinter and pager signals; U.S. unmanned aerial vehicle datalink signals (for the HUNTER and PREDATOR UAVs); and the Joint Air to Surface Stand Off Missile (JASSM) datalink. The PRC is known to use two of the signals resident in LUNCHBOX. Additionally, LUNCHBOX contained detailed working aids for 29 of the 40 PROFORMA signals.

(S//SI) Two PROFORMA-related USSIDs (212 and 342) –stored on electronic media that was possibly compromised– and several working aids provided detail about Russian-designed PROFORMA signals used by North Korea, Russia, Vietnam, and possibly the PRC. This material detailed the association of signals to specific weapon systems.

4.2.2.2 (U) MARTES

TOP SECRET//COMINT//NOFORN//X1

TOP SECRET//COMINT//NOFORN//X1

(S) MARTES is the name of a set of software tools for collecting, analyzing, and processing signals and was loaded on a laptop computer. A new version of MARTES is released approximately every six months, and it is generally divided into COMINT, FISINT, and ELINT tools. The COMINT version (1999.0.2) of MARTES was used for this deployment and was classified TOP SECRET//COMINT. It contained source code, executable, help, signal parameter files, tutorials, and sample signals. Some of the sample signals were simulated data while others were real-world intercept.

(S) The MARTES laptop also included a Radio Signals Notation (RASIN) Manual, RASIN Working Aid, and associated materials. Together, the RASIN manual and the aforementioned files provided a comprehensive overview of how the U.S. Cryptologic System exploits an adversary's signal environment.

(S//SI) A portable, digital player/recorder used to collect the signals analyzed by MARTES contained a tape of 45 minutes of enciphered and unenciphered PRC Navy communications. The unenciphered portions carried speech segments that identified PRC communicants. When emergency destruction procedures caused the recorder to lose power, the tape was locked in the recorder's drive. The digital recorder was returned on the recovered EP-3E; however, the tape had been removed.

4.2.2.3 (U) Other COMINT Equipment

(C) In addition to the carry-on SCARAB computer and MARTES laptop, other COMINT equipment included the integrated COMINT collection system and the COMINT Supervisor's laptop computer.

(S) The integrated COMINT collection system onboard the EP-3E consisted of antiquated HF, VHF, and UHF receivers, a rudimentary signal distribution network, and narrowband cassette recorders. The COMINT collection system used the ALD-9 antenna and processor package. System display and control terminals did not have the capacity to store classified COMINT information. This equipment suite contained no sensitive technologies, and presents no compromise concern. The COMINT Supervisor's laptop contained technical data, USSIDs, and other COMINT documentation.

4.2.3 (U) Documentation

4.2.3.1 (U) USSIDs

(C) Twenty-three United States Signals Intelligence Directives (USSIDs) or excerpts of USSIDs were onboard the EP-3E, either in hardcopy or on electronic media (see Appendix B for a complete listing). USSIDs are directives issued by DIRNSA as official policy documents governing SIGINT activities and resources. Separate series of USSIDs cover basic SIGINT guidance; collection; processing of raw intercept data; requirements, reporting and distribution; and tasking for specific cryptologic activities.

TOP SECRET//COMINT//NOFORN//X1

TOP SECRET//COMINT//NOFORN//X1

4.2.3.2 (U) COMINT Documentation

(S//SI) EP-3E cryptologic technicians had a variety of technical aids, tasking documents, and SIGINT governing documents to assist them in collecting PRC tactical communications from coastal and inland units in the South China Sea. This documentation outlined specific PRC units of interest to the U.S. and provided detailed information on Signals Operating Instructions (e.g., target frequencies, call signs), order of battle, and the periodicity at which this data is to be collected. This information was in hardcopy format, in documents such as the Intercept Tasking Database and Collection Requirements Number tasking messages.

(C) Additionally, working aids and technical notes provided detailed background data on target emitters. Several crew members also carried their individual JQRs for training and proficiency purposes. For cryptologic trainees, a completed JQR would provide specific, classified knowledge of an Area of Operations, e.g., the Far East Asian Region, and general knowledge of cryptologic functions such as collecting and processing SIGINT data.

4.2.4 (U//FOUO) COMINT Equipment Damage Assessment

4.2.4.1 (U) LUNCHBOX PROFORMA Processor

(S) The overall damage from the compromise of the LUNCHBOX processor is considered medium. PRC exploitation of the LUNCHBOX processor would enable them to process PROFORMA in the same manner as the U.S. This analysis would provide the PRC with an understanding of U.S. capabilities against PROFORMA signals and could lead to an understanding of U.S. capabilities in other signals analysis areas.

(S) Examination of the recovered LUNCHBOX processor revealed that, while externally the recovered drive appeared to be in good condition, internally the hard drive platters were destroyed. Laboratory reenactment of the crew's LUNCHBOX destruction attempts produced no damage to the hard drive. Therefore, the crew's actions are assessed not to have caused the damage. We believe the PRC shattered the hard drives after exploiting them. (For a discussion of the laboratory destruction testing at the Aberdeen Test Center, see Appendix D.) Though the PRC returned the LUNCHBOX processor, two unique signals processing circuit boards necessary for the LUNCHBOX to process PROFORMA signals were missing. All data and software on the LUNCHBOX processor are considered compromised.

(S//SI) The PRC's most effective denial methods would be to move from current over-the-air transmissions to landline transmissions, or to more advanced radio communications techniques, such as frequency hopping, that could complicate the U.S. Cryptologic System's exploitation efforts. The PRC could also potentially deny future access by encrypting these signals, although encryption is not likely. PROFORMA signals are not routinely encrypted because of their perishable nature and the requirement to provide fast, dependable data throughput. However, some PROFORMA signals are

TOP SECRET//COMINT//NOFORN//X1

TOP SECRET//COMINT//NOFORN//X1

carried within other encrypted communication signals and that practice could be increased. These changes, especially if shared with other countries such as Cuba, Egypt, Iran, Russia, and Vietnam, could significantly impact U.S. SIGINT support to deployed U.S. and allied forces.

(C) Damage from the compromise of the HUNTER and PREDATOR UAV datalink signals and the Joint Air-to-Surface Stand-off Missile (JASSM) seeker video datalink signal is assessed to be low. These datalink signals are broadcast in the clear and are unclassified.

(S) In addition to PROFORMA processing software, other signal analysis tools were loaded on the SCARAB computer. While these tools represent valuable capabilities to the U.S. Cryptologic System, they are all based on open source techniques. Potential damage from this compromise is low.

4.2.4.2   (U) MARTES

(S) The overall damage from compromised information on the MARTES laptop is considered medium. The MARTES laptop sustained no visible damage (Figure 3), but its recovered hard drives were found to be shattered. Technical experts assess that the crew did not cause this damage. Based on all available data, we believe that the PRC copied the laptop's hard drives and then destroyed them. All data resident on the MARTES laptop, including signal identification and processing software, working aids, and signal samples, is considered compromised.

Figure 3
(C) Recovered MARTES Laptop

(S) Two factors establish the assessment of this loss as medium: (1) the laptop included signal-specific processing capabilities, and (2) the laptop had source code, help files, samples and tutorials that could enable the PRC to extend and modify the capabilities of the compromised signals analysis tools. Of particular note is that some of the signal-specific processing capabilities were designed to target PRC systems.

(S) Compromised capabilities provide the PRC with a comprehensive understanding of the level of U.S. signals analysis expertise as of early 1999. The key factor that limits the severity of the compromise to medium is that these capabilities will

TOP SECRET//COMINT//NOFORN//X1

TOP SECRET//COMINT//NOFORN//X1

not allow the PRC to make any advances in exploiting U.S. encryption systems, nor will it allow the PRC to discover flaws in the protection of its own communications.

(S) Modernized equipments would likely have prevented this compromise. Computerizing the recording capabilities and providing built-in encryption would eliminate the use of tape and the associated need for physical destruction.

(S) Additionally, the depth of signal processing capabilities provided by MARTES was not required for this mission. A tailored system designed to focus on rapid signals detection, identification, collection, and processing is more appropriate to the mission.

4.2.4.3 (U) Other COMINT Equipment

(S//SI) Damage from the compromise of the EP-3E's integrated COMINT collection suite is considered low. The rudimentary nature of the system components will not provide the PRC with any substantial information on the U.S. ability to exploit any signals other than basic non-enciphered tactical communications. The fact that U.S. SRO assets collect tactical communications on PRC targets is already known to the PRC. The PRC could attempt to reverse engineer the ALD-9 antenna and processor system, but information and specifications on more capable systems is readily available in open source literature.

(S) No physical destruction was performed on integrated COMINT equipment due to the unavailability of proper destruction devices. The crew did zeroize all receivers and partially purge the master system display and control terminal. In addition, cassette tapes were extracted from narrowband recorders, stretched, and possibly torn. These tapes remained on the aircraft.

(C) Damage from the compromise of the COMINT Supervisor's laptop is considered low, due to the significant damage inflicted by the crew. Although the damage was severe, the PRC's ability to recover data from the hard drive cannot be ruled out. Damage from the possible compromise of USSIDs and other documentation on this laptop is discussed below in Section 4.2.5.

4.2.5 (U) COMINT Documentation Damage Assessment

(S//SI) The compromise of the largely tactical COMINT documentation is rated medium. The most sensitive and damaging documentation compromised was contained in collection requirements hardcopy documents that detail U.S. tasking against PRC military datalink and microwave signals. The tasking data, containing information such as frequencies, data rates, dish sizes, and target communicants, outlined the U.S. capability to exploit digital signals. However, U.S. national collection systems were not referenced.

4.2.5.1 (U) Technical COMINT Documentation

TOP SECRET//COMINT//NOFORN//X1

(S//SI) The U.S. ability to collect PRC submarine signal transmissions and make subsequent vessel correlations was compromised. This compromise could prompt the PRC to modify the signal that the U.S. exploits to make vessel correlations. Although its ability to exploit these signals is limited, NSA is confident that the U.S. Cryptologic System could recover from any changes to the signal content. Compromised documents further revealed U.S. direction finding capabilities against PRC submarines. The PRC could respond by employing COMSEC to elude U.S. direction finding. Further, PRC communications equipment modifications could complicate NSA's exploitation efforts. The overall impact of this compromise is assessed to be medium.

(S//SI) Crew training materials also compromised U.S. knowledge of the PRC's Submarine Launched Ballistic Missile (SLBM) program. The information outlined the SLBM program's organization, platforms, missile testing operations, and communications. Although the PRC probably believed that the U.S. possessed this information, it was probably not aware that the information could be derived from SIGINT collection and analysis. PRC efforts to deny the U.S. future information on this program could be overcome by U.S. cryptologic sources and techniques. Therefore the impact of this compromise is assessed to be medium.

(S//SI) Also potentially damaging are compromised tasking documents that referred to an advanced PRC communications system currently under development. The PRC could respond by modifying the new system or implementing more rigorous COMSEC procedures potentially denying the U.S. future insight. Additionally, realizing that the U.S. has a means for acquiring data on one of its systems before it is operationally deployed could prompt the PRC to tighten security in its defense industry institutes to include COMSEC enhancements. The impact of this compromise is assessed to be medium.

(S//SI) The potential damage from the compromise of Signals Operating Instructions is assessed to be low. PRC analysis of this data could reveal in part the extent to which the U.S. can and does exploit PRC military tactical communications. As a result, the PRC could change its use of frequencies or call signs, or could move to deny future airborne platforms access by changing operating times. Frequency and call sign changes occur with regular periodicity, e.g., monthly, quarterly, annually, and are a standard operating procedure. Therefore, changes of this type are factored into NSA's ability to satisfy customer requirements. Of note is that the PRC has not implemented a major communications change in 15 to 20 years (see discussion in Section 6.2.1).

(S//SI) A mid- to long-term possibility is that the PRC could upgrade its communications equipments to more advanced signaling systems (e.g., frequency hopping systems), or it could increase the use of encryption in its communications. The PRC, as is the case with almost all countries, is constantly upgrading and evolving its communications capabilities so an eventual migration to more advanced signals can be anticipated. Incorporating widespread encryption into tactical communications equipments is costly and cumbersome, and therefore not believed to be a likely outcome of the EP-3E compromise.

(S//SI) The extent to which compromised JQRs were completed by individual crew members varied from little to very extensive detail. The most revealing and potentially damaging JQR materials compromised were completed JQRs and study guides for the PRC Navy Operator and COMEVAL positions. These JQR materials detailed specific target information (e.g., frequencies, units of interest) and described U.S. reconnaissance operating areas, programs, and collection platforms.

4.2.5.2 (U) USSIDs

(S//SI) While overall impact from the compromise of SIGINT directives carried on the EP-3E is low, three compromised directives are of concern. Of immediate concern is the known compromise of a hardcopy of USSID 5511, which details instructions and information on COMINT Advisory Support to Sensitive Reconnaissance Operations (NICKELBACK conditions). While this compromise will not affect the U.S. ability to perform SRO missions, the PRC could take action to deceive the SIGINT system by transmitting false information, causing the SIGINT system to provide mission aircraft with incorrect NICKELBACK conditions. Actual spoofing –imitating U.S. communications to pass false advisory support to an SRO platform– is extremely unlikely, since it would require the PRC to have both U.S. communications gear and daily crypto. NSA has evaluated this possibility and concludes that there are sufficient monitoring assets to readily detect any such denial and deception actions and to advise an SRO platform.

Figure 4
(C) Recovered COMINT Supervisor's Laptop

(S//SI) The possible recovery of USSIDs 107 and 303 from the damaged COMINT Supervisor's laptop (Figure 4) is of concern. USSID 107, which focuses on special signals recognition and reporting procedures, reveals that the U.S. has the capability to identify and collect special PRC signals. Coupled with other compromised SOI data, this compromise would confirm the U.S. ability to monitor special signals transmitted by PRC submarines. Any SOI changes in these transmissions could result in significant damage; therefore, this potential compromise is assessed to be medium.

TOP SECRET//COMINT//NOFORN//X1

USSID 303 (SIGINT Reporters' Instructions) specifies SIGINT interest in the PRC, North Korea, the Philippines, Cambodia, Vietnam, and Thailand. The PRC's disclosure of this information could have political implications (see Cryptologic Foreign Partner Impact, Section 6.3) and could lead to SOI changes in these nations. The damage resulting from this potential compromise is assessed as low.

4.2.6 (U) Recommendations

- (U//FOUO) Limit classified and sensitive materials carried onboard SRO platforms to mission-essential materials only. Minimize hardcopy materials in favor of electronic media.
- (U//FOUO) Identify computer hard drives for priority destruction and/or jettison. Mark hard drives with a location for striking to ensure physical destruction.
- (U//FOUO) Eliminate source code from fielded software.
- (U//FOUO) Eliminate tape-based recording, replacing it with computer-based recorders with built-in encryption.
- (S) Remove processing capability for the HUNTER and PREDATOR UAV and JASSM datalink signals from LUNCHBOX.
- (S) Provide a tailored signals processing capability that fully meets mission requirements for rapid signal detection and identification.
- (U//FOUO) Replace the SCARAB computer key-lock mechanism with a manual quick-release bolt.
- (C) Review compromised USSID material to determine if there is a need to change, modify, or update any USSID.
- (S//SI) Continue to monitor PRC communications for evidence of denial and deception activities related to SRO missions.

4.3 (U) ELINT Equipment and Documentation

(C) This section focuses on the compromised ELINT equipments and related ELINT working aids and notes.

4.3.1 (U) Findings

- (C) The EP-3E's installed ELINT equipment was not destroyed.
- (C) Most classified ELINT documentation was compromised.
- (C) All data on the ELINT Evaluator's laptop computer, including a comprehensive ELINT Order of Battle, was compromised.
- (S) The primary impact of the compromise of ELINT documentation would be in improved PRC electronic warfare planning against the U.S. and Taiwan.

4.3.2 (U) ELINT Equipment

TOP SECRET//COMINT//NOFORN//X1

TOP SECRET//COMINT//NOFORN//X1

(S//NF) The ELINT systems onboard the EP-3E include a disparate collection of antennas, signal distribution networks, wideband and narrowband receivers, recorders, and processing and display equipment. The bulk of these systems are off-the-shelf devices that, although designed for the ELINT mission, contain no particularly sensitive technologies. Those systems that represent a specific concern include the AN/ULQ-16 and the AN/ALQ-108. The AN/ULQ-16 is a computerized pulse processor used to make detailed timing measurements of radar signals. The AN/ALQ-108 is an enemy IFF interrogation system used to actively and passively exploit early Soviet IFF and range extension signals.

(C) Emergency destruction of the installed ELINT equipment by the crew was largely ineffective. The crew did zeroize all memories and erase all mission data, but the rugged construction of critical components and lack of destruction tools prevented adequate destruction. The limited damage to this equipment can be circumvented by a competent reverse engineering effort. It is assessed that all ELINT hardware systems on the aircraft have been fully compromised.

4.3.3   (U) ELINT Documentation

(C) Most classified ELINT documentation was compromised. This documentation included the EPL (ELINT Parameter Limits), CTEGM (Collector Technical ELINT Guidance Manual), and a HULTEC (Hull-to-Emitter Correlation) database, and miscellaneous notes on PRC and Russian ships and weapon systems. One document described the tactical employment of the AN/ULQ-16 and discussed radar fingerprinting techniques and procedures. Equipment maintenance documentation and wiring diagrams intended for in-flight troubleshooting also remained onboard.

(S) The ELINT Evaluator's laptop was left onboard and is considered compromised. The laptop contained a comprehensive (worldwide) Electronic Order of Battle (EOB). Information included locations and names of fixed radar sites, along with designations of radar systems installed at these sites. Information in the database was limited to the SECRET level. One file discussed the purpose and employment of the AN/ALQ-108 and identified similar equipment as being deployed on two U.S. aircraft, the E-3 AWACS and F-15 Eagle.

4.3.4   (U) ELINT Damage Assessment

(S) The potential damage from the compromise of ELINT data is assessed to be medium. The EPL reveals the sum of U.S. knowledge at the Secret-level about the parameters and operating characteristics of most known radars from both U.S. and foreign manufacturers. Signals described range from air traffic control and early warning radars to airborne intercept radars and cruise missile seekers. Included are details of U.S. and allied systems (although not wartime reserve modes), including most equipment employed by Taiwan. National-level associations with ELINT collection were not compromised.

TOP SECRET//COMINT//NOFORN//X1

(S) The CTEGM details specific gaps in U.S. ELINT knowledge. It tasks collection against (and thus identifies) suspected wartime reserve modes and poorly understood operating modes of foreign emitters. It identifies knowledge gaps for both radar and PROFORMA systems. Exploitation of the EPL and CTEGM could facilitate PRC electronic warfare planning against the U.S., India, and Taiwan, and allow the employment of denial and deception techniques tailored to U.S. knowledge gaps.

(S) The HULTEC database equates precise radar timing measurements (such as those provided by the AN/ULQ-16) to individual PRC ships and submarines. Exploitation could allow the PRC to implement changes to shipborne radars that could temporarily deny the U.S. identification of naval vessels through ELINT.

(S) Exploitation of the EOB could provide the PRC with insights into the accuracy and extent of U.S. knowledge about PRC radars and early warning networks. Analysis could reveal the fact of U.S. shortcomings in the ability to produce high quality information on PRC early warning networks and U.S. uncertainty in identifying certain types of radars. However, the PRC would not be able to determine the full extent of U.S. knowledge concerning PRC radar installations since the compromised EOB was limited in depth.

(S) The technologies resident in compromised ELINT systems would not advance present PRC technical capabilities. PRC radar and ELINT technologies are advanced to the point that they are capable of employing all techniques used on the EP-3E. The primary impact of the compromise of these systems would be in the operational lessons the PRC learns about U.S. ELINT techniques and procedures. These lessons, if properly applied, could help the PRC counter U.S. collection efforts as well as improve its tactical ELINT collection.

(S) Analysis of the recovered AN/ALQ-108 reveals that it was thoroughly examined by PRC engineers. While the AN/ALQ-108 is technically incapable of exploiting PRC IFF signals, PRC analysis could reveal that such a capability is easily within U.S. reach (other U.S. assets are able to exploit PRC IFF signals, and similar efforts are ongoing). The most likely effects would be increased IFF signals security and an acceleration of PRC procurement of more advanced IFF equipment.

4.3.5 (U) Recommendations

(U//FOUO) The first two recommendations in Section 4.2.6 regarding limiting classified and sensitive materials and identifying computer hard drives for destruction, among others, apply to ELINT equipment and documentation.

4.4 (U) SIGINT Configuration and Materials Management

(C) As this report details, numerous factors contributed to the compromise of SIGINT data. The damage from this incident would have been significantly lessened if

TOP SECRET//COMINT//NOFORN//X1

there existed a unifying cryptologic strategy for preventing information from falling into an adversary's possession. Such a strategy exists in Information Assurance (IA), where it is assumed that COMSEC equipments will be compromised. The triad of controlled equipment, encrypted communications, and robust key management significantly mitigates the damage incurred through the loss or compromise of any single COMSEC element (see section 5.2). Conversely, SIGINT is founded on a "no compromise" principle. SIGINT is to be protected at all times and, if it is deemed to be in jeopardy of compromise or loss, destroyed. This approach lacks flexibility and reflects an era when SIGINT capabilities resided on hardware and in hardcopy versus today's world where increasingly these capabilities reside in software.

(C) If SIGINT data cannot be protected or destroyed, then the amount of material at risk should be minimized by the use of effective controls. This did not occur. SIGINT equipments and materials were provided to the EP-3E mission in a haphazard manner Although SIGINT materials are among the most sensitive in the Intelligence Community, there was a lack of control and oversight of both hardcopy and softcopy items. Software was disseminated that contained unnecessary files, including programming source code. Additionally, there was a lack of guidance regarding SIGINT equipments, software versions, and documentation allowed onboard the platform. Adequate inventories of SIGINT materials were not maintained and the crew was allowed to carry excessive and unnecessary SIGINT materials onboard.

(C) The immediate development and implementation of a governing strategy for deployable SIGINT equipment and materials is paramount. As the U.S. Cryptologic System moves toward placing more and increasingly sensitive SIGINT capabilities in the field, new safeguard capabilities are required not only for SRO platforms, but for all SIGINT collection activities potentially at risk.

4.4.1 (U) Recommendations

- (U//FOUO) Work with industry and the Intelligence Community to develop and implement safeguard capabilities for SIGINT equipment and materials used by SRO platforms and other SIGINT collection activities at risk.
- (U//FOUO) Develop and implement configuration controls to govern the use of NSA-deployed software versions and maintain cognizance of field modifications; include procedures to annually overwrite all software with the most currently available software.

TOP SECRET//COMINT//NOFORN//X1

5.0 (U) IA Review and Assessment

5.1 (U) Key Findings

- (S) Overall damage resulting from the compromise of cryptographic equipments and materials is assessed to be low.
- (S) The greatest potential for PRC COMSEC gains is in the area of analyzing and potentially emulating U.S. COMSEC tradecraft.

5.2 (U) Cryptographic Tutorial

(S) U.S. cryptologic equipment contains complex mathematical encryption algorithms or cryptographic logic. Most U.S. cryptographic systems are designed for multiple operating environments, including tactical, and it is assumed from the day the equipment is issued that it eventually will fall into enemy hands.

(S) Cryptographic devices are designed so that the cryptographically significant portion of the encryption process can be changed frequently, normally once per day. The variability takes the form of a stream of random numbers called key. The key basically tells the built-in encryption system how to vary itself with each character transmitted. The NSA design philosophy prevents our adversaries from reading U.S. communications without the key, even if they have obtained the logic and message traffic, provided the cryptographic system is employed properly.

5.3 (U) Cryptographic Materials and Equipments

5.3.1 (U) Findings

- (S) Though most (estimated 95%) of the sensitive COMSEC materials (keys and codebooks) onboard were jettisoned, the limited amount of keying materials that remained onboard were compromised.
- (C) COMSEC equipments and material carried onboard the mission aircraft exceeded mission needs.
- (C) An accurate inventory of COMSEC material and devices on the mission aircraft was difficult to obtain in a timely manner.
- (S) The crew zeroized all cryptographic devices left onboard.
- (S) The crew did not destroy the cryptographic equipments left onboard.
- (S) All communications keying materials, except for the Global Positioning System (GPS) worldwide key, were superseded within 15 hours of the EP-3E's landing in the PRC. The GPS worldwide key was superseded by 12 April 2001.
- (S) All the cryptographic equipments left onboard have been previously compromised, though not directly to the PRC.

TOP SECRET//COMINT//NOFORN//X1

TOP SECRET//COMINT//NOFORN//X1

- (S) Some Pacific theater communications from late March to early April could be vulnerable to PRC decryption efforts if the PRC is able to exploit or reconstruct the keying material left onboard the EP-3E.

5.3.2 (U) Damage Assessment

(S) The EP-3E carried the complete complement of COMSEC equipments and keying materials necessary to conduct its SRO mission, including several KY-58 secure voice and KG-84 secure data devices (Figure 5), KYK-13 and KOI-18 electronic fill devices, a KL-43 off-line encryption device, and a Global Positioning System (GPS) unit. The EP-3E also carried keying and other cryptographic materials for its various secure devices (see Appendix B for a complete list of equipments and cryptographic material onboard). Top Secret keying material in canisters, entire codebooks, and call sign lists were onboard. In all, the EP-3E carried COMSEC materials in excess of what was needed for the mission. Nearly a month's worth of keying material and codebook pages were carried that were not scheduled to become effective until well after the scheduled landing. COMSEC devices onboard included unused electronic fill devices and several installed spare encryption devices.

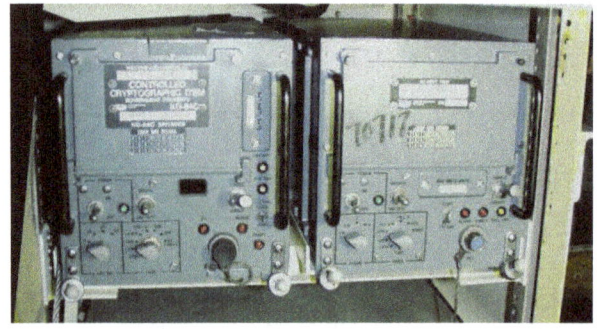 

Figure 5
(C) Typical KG-84 and KY-58 Devices

(S) The use of an electronic key loading device such as the CYZ-10 Data Transfer Device (DTD) can eliminate the risk of hardcopy keying material compromise. These devices can hold multiple keys, load multiple devices, and are easily zeroized. DTDs were in the EP-3E inventory but were not carried on the mission aircraft. Had the crew loaded the key into the DTD and left the key tape at the staging base, destruction of the key would have been easily and quickly accomplished.

(S//NF) Overall damage from compromised EP-3E cryptographic materials is assessed to be low due in part to the action of the crew and the supersession of keying material at risk. All of the compromised keying materials were superseded within 15 hours except for the GPS worldwide key that was superseded by 12 April. The cryptographic equipments onboard were either jettisoned or zeroized.

5.3.3 (U) Cryptographic Materials

TOP SECRET//COMINT//NOFORN//X1

TOP SECRET//COMINT//NOFORN//X1

(S//NF) After the flight station regained control of the EP-3E, the crew began emergency destruction of cryptographic materials (e.g., fill devices, keys, and codebooks). The crew jettisoned three of the four fill devices (i.e., the KYK-13s and KOI-18s), key tape canisters, and codebooks in a COMSEC Material System (CMS) box (see Figure 6). Materials not jettisoned included 16 specific cryptographic keys and

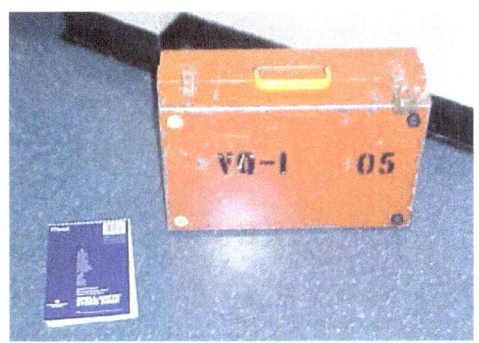

Figure 6
(U) Typical CMS Box

codebooks, a KOI-18, and a KL-43. Before departing the aircraft, the crew hand tore the paper materials and spread them throughout the aircraft. However, since the paper materials were not destroyed with approved equipment such as a crosscut shredder, the PRC would probably be able to reconstruct the key tape. U.S. experts have demonstrated the ability to reconstruct tape from pieces torn as the crew described. Examination of the recovered EP-3E revealed that some torn keying material was retained by the PRC.

(S) Compromised keying material was limited to Pacific network controlling authorities and the GPS worldwide key. NSA ensured that all non-GPS key was superseded in less than 15 hours. The GPS worldwide key, controlled by U.S. SPACECOM, was superseded by 12 April 2001. During this 11-day period, the GPS system was potentially vulnerable to PRC exploitation. The GPS key is used to authenticate GPS data for the user and the PRC could have potentially used the compromised key to spoof or mislead system users. However, no anomalies were noted during the timeframe. GPS key supersession required 11 days because of the key's global nature (250,000 end users and some foreign partner use) and the challenges associated with this first-ever global supersession. U.S. SPACECOM's lessons learned from European operations in the past two years were instrumental in supporting the massive supersession of the GPS worldwide key. The primary lesson learned by SPACECOM was to have follow-on editions of GPS key pre-positioned to support supersession.

5.3.4 (U) Cryptographic Equipments

(TS) Sixteen cryptographic devices remained onboard the EP-3E. All of these devices, i.e., KG-84s and KY-58s, were zeroized but not physically destroyed. During zeroization, all traces of the 128-bit key are removed from storage of any register or

TOP SECRET//COMINT//NOFORN//X1

TOP SECRET//COMINT//NOFORN//X1

memory. This process, which involves the multiple overwriting of memory registers with 1's and 0's, is 100 percent effective in rendering the data unrecoverable.

(S) There were no maintenance manuals or other supporting documentation onboard the EP-3E that could aid the PRC in exploitation efforts. These are controlled items and were not required for this SRO mission.

(S) All of the cryptographic devices that remained onboard the EP-3E have been previously compromised, though not directly to the PRC. However, there is strong evidence that the PRC has aggressively sought to obtain these equipments. Also of note is that some of these devices, for example components of KG-84 devices, have been available on popular Internet auction sites.

(S//SI) Compromised cryptographic materials might enable PRC SIGINT units to decrypt limited U.S. Pacific area encrypted transmissions for 31 March and 1 April. Since the PRC possessed the crypto-device from the EP-3E, they would have been able to decrypt communications if they had:
- Recorded and retained the communications for future exploitation, and
- Located and reconstructed the keying material that was hand torn and left onboard the aircraft.

(S//SI) If the PRC succeeded in this regard, they would have been able to read those encrypted Pacific area communications passed on 31 March and 1 April using the same key compromised from the EP-3E. To determine the extent of potential damage, NSA contacted the Pacific (network) Controlling Authorities to ascertain what communications were transmitted during these two days. Pacific Controlling Authority responses indicated that because this was a weekend, there was minimal data transmitted. Communications susceptible to decryption over this period were limited to low-level, perishable tactical reports such as KLIEGLIGHTs and TACREPs. The assessment is that this data would be of little benefit to the PRC.

5.3.5 (U) Recommendations

- (U//FOUO) Limit COMSEC materials and cryptologic devices onboard deployed platforms to those required to accomplish the platform's mission in a specific timeframe and in a given area of responsibility.
- (U//FOUO) Use electronic key loading devices and leave hardcopy key tape and canisters at the staging base.
- (U//FOUO) Maintain a comprehensive and readily available inventory of all field-deployed COMSEC materials and cryptologic devices.
- (U//FOUO) Maintain destruction records and supersession messages at the staging base.
- (U//FOUO) Continue to refine procedures for timely supersession of GPS worldwide key.
- (U//FOUO) Make crosscut shredders available for emergency destruction of keying material.

TOP SECRET//COMINT//NOFORN//X1

TOP SECRET//COMINT//NOFORN//X1

5.4 (U) Potential for PRC Intelligence Gain from IA Compromises

(TS) The greatest potential for PRC intelligence gain from the loss of U.S. cryptographic information is in the area of implementation security. The U.S. incorporates high quality randomization and strong fail-safe designs into its keying material and cryptographic devices. These security measures protect encrypted U.S. communications from decryption attacks. If PRC technicians successfully exploit the compromised EP-3E cryptographic material and devices, they would gain information as to how the U.S. incorporates these security designs. This insight could provide the PRC with an impetus to incorporate similar designs in its indigenous cryptographic materials and devices, making U.S. decryption efforts more difficult.

TOP SECRET//COMINT//NOFORN//X1

6.0 (U) PRC Potential Actions and the Cryptologic Response

6.1 (U) Key Finding

- (C) The overall potential foreign relations impact from compromise of materials onboard the EP-3E is assessed to be low.

(S) This section reviews potential PRC actions and the U.S. Cryptologic System response, including the SIGINT collection strategy in the wake of the incident and cryptologic foreign partner impact. It also reviews counterintelligence issues, the potential for recovery of jettisoned equipment, and PRC interaction with the crew.

6.2 (U) SIGINT Collection Strategy

(S//SI) NSA does not anticipate major PRC communications procedure changes as a result of U.S. SIGINT data compromised on the EP-3E aircraft grounded on Hainan Island 1 April 2001. One potential result of the compromise might be a PRC decision to accelerate implementation of planned communications upgrades (such as a transition to fiber and increased use of encryption) or changes to communications Signals Operation Instructions (SOI).

6.2.1 (U) PRC Military Communications

(S//SI) The PRC military does not generally implement nationwide SOI changes at once; each service implements SOI changes according to its own plans, and tends not to adhere to a regular schedule. The last nationwide SOI change occurred over a two-year period in the early 1980s and it took NSA several months to re-establish continuity on the target. To date, recovery of that call sign allocation system is still incomplete, however, this does not affect target continuity or reporting. The most recent smaller scale SOI change occurred between December 2000 and February 2001, and NSA has almost completely recovered the changes. If the PRC implements new PLA-wide call sign systems, it could take from several months to a few years to recover the SOI for general PRC military operations completely, especially for PRC ground forces.

(S//SI) The PRC regularly uses Denial and Deception (D&D) techniques. As a result of the compromise of tactical SIGINT information, the PRC could be prompted to take action to deny U.S. collection of PLA communications. One means of detecting PRC D&D efforts would be to employ covert collection assets during SRO missions. These platforms could then monitor PLA communications for departures from the norm while SRO missions are flying in the area.

(S) Any PRC denial or deception effort would likely affect more than just the U.S. Cryptologic System. U.S. foreign cryptologic partners using similar SIGINT sources and methods would be impacted if the PRC implements communications changes as a result of the compromise.

TOP SECRET//COMINT//NOFORN//X1

TOP SECRET//COMINT//NOFORN//X1

(S) NSA does not expect the PRC to make major changes in its military radars and usage, because of the prohibitive expense of refitting all of its aircraft, naval combatants, and coastal defense units. However, it would not be unusual for the PRC to modify some of the signal parameters on its military radars. If the PRC changes ELINT signal parameters, complete recovery would take relatively little time –probably a few days– but would be labor intensive, since each entity would have to be analyzed and recovered separately. NSA monitoring of PRC communications would also reveal changes in the target's air surveillance PROFORMA signals. The rapidity of recovery from a change would depend upon the extent of PRC signal modifications.

6.2.2 (U) PRC Non-military Communications

(S//SI) Intelligence on PRC non-military targets is gleaned from a wide variety of collection sources, none of which is likely to be affected by the compromises associated with the PRC's ability to exploit the collection systems and working aids onboard the EP-3E mission aircraft.

6.3 (U) Cryptologic Foreign Partner Impact

6.3.1 (U) Findings

- (C) The EP-3E carried no data that would reveal Second or Third Party sources or methods.
- (C) Tactical Signals Operating Instructions that enabled cryptologic technicians to monitor allied airspace for situational awareness and safety of transit purposes were compromised.
- (C) One of the EP-3E's avionics systems, the AN/ULQ-16 radar pulse processor that is used by several foreign partners, was compromised.
- (S//SI) The compromised LUNCHBOX PROFORMA processor (see Section 4.2) included weapons systems command and control signaling information of foreign partners.
- (S) The compromised ELINT Parameters List included detailed emitter parameters for many radars and weapons systems of foreign partners.
- (S) The compromised ELINT Order of Battle included information on foreign partners' radar systems.
- (TS//SI) U.S. cryptologic relationships with the United Kingdom, Australia, Japan, South Korea, Taiwan and Thailand were identified in crew technical notes. Although the relationships with the UK and Australia are unclassified, the fact of relationships with Japan, South Korea, and Thailand are classified SECRET//COMINT and the fact of a relationship with Taiwan is classified TOP SECRET//COMINT.

6.3.2 (U) Introduction

TOP SECRET//COMINT//NOFORN//X1

(S) Several cryptologic foreign partner relationships were compromised to the PRC. These losses are not judged to be significant, however, and the overall potential foreign relations impact of the compromised EP-3E materials is assessed to be low. Information on cryptologic foreign partner impacts and notification strategy is located in Appendix C.

(TS//SI) Compromised information included data acknowledging U.S. cryptologic relationships with Taiwan, Japan, South Korea, and Thailand; SOI related to the airspace of some partners, such as Taiwan; and PROFORMA data from some partner countries. This information was located onboard the EP-3E in software tools and hardcopy notes used by the cryptologic technicians. Information such as SOI enabled the aircraft to transit safely to its area of responsibility, conduct its mission, and return safely to its staging base. Other information was used to exploit communications of the PRC and several neighboring countries.

6.3.3 (U) Second and Third Party Disclosures

(TS//SI) The EP-3E carried no materials that would jeopardize any Second or Third Party sources and methods. U.S. cryptologic relationships with the United Kingdom, Australia, Japan, South Korea, Taiwan and Thailand were identified and compromised in crew technical notes. Although the relationships with the UK and Australia are unclassified, the fact of relationships with Japan, South Korea, and Thailand is classified SECRET//COMINT and the fact of a relationship with Taiwan is classified TOP SECRET//COMINT. Crew notes also compromised the relationship between the U.S. and Japanese airborne reconnaissance programs.

(S//SI) One of the duties of the EP-3E's technicians was to support the safe transit of the aircraft to its area of responsibility through the monitoring of friendly and potentially unfriendly communications and radar. To accomplish this task, the aircraft carried significant technical data on target nations such as Russia, North Korea, and Vietnam, as well as data on friendly nations such as Taiwan. The aircraft's cryptologic technicians monitored Taiwanese tactical communications to provide situational awareness data to the EP-3E's cockpit crew as necessary.

(S) Compromised technical information included PROFORMA data for nearly 50 nations. Additionally, the Electronic Order of Battle (EOB) database carried on the EP-3E provided information on the location, number, and type of radars worldwide. The EOB did not, however, contain parametric data (e.g., frequency, pulse information, power levels).

6.3.4 (U) Disclosure Impact

(TS//SI) The U.S. government's intelligence relationship with the UK and Australian government is unclassified, and the fact that U.S. reconnaissance aircraft monitor the external environment, e.g., Taiwan, for safe transit purposes is not a major

TOP SECRET//COMINT//NOFORN//X1

cause for concern by U.S. partners or allies. The potential impact of the compromise of the relationship between Japan and the U.S. EP-3E program (U.S. aircraft stage from Japanese territory) is considered to be low. We assess the impact of compromising U.S. relationships with South Korea and Taiwan as low for similar reasons. Regarding the U.S. relationship with Thailand, the impact of that compromise is also considered low, given the lack of any U.S. basing in country and the overt landing of U.S. reconnaissance aircraft in Thailand.

(S) As it pertains to the EP-3E platform, the potential impact of the compromise of avionics systems and its impact on foreign relations is assessed to be low. The AN/ULQ-16, a radar pulse processor, was the only compromised system known to be in use by foreign nations. This early 1980s vintage system employs techniques similar to those now common in commercial telephony applications. Australia, Taiwan, Japan, South Korea, Italy and Norway are among the nations that still use this system. The AN/ULQ-16 is designed to analyze the pulse characteristics of radars, and is particularly well suited for older tactical systems still widely used in the Former Soviet Union, the PRC, and Korea.

(S//SI) The potential impact from PRC disclosure of the LUNCHBOX data to other countries is a concern. From a SIGINT perspective, the PRC's exploitation of LUNCHBOX and the disclosure of its PROFORMA capabilities to foreign partners could result in a loss of access to some foreign PROFORMA signals by the U.S. and its allies (see section 4.2). From a foreign relations perspective, the fact that the U.S. has the ability to monitor the command and control environment of friendly and unfriendly nations would be of minor concern to some countries. NSA has developed notification procedures and will coordinate notification of foreign partners with appropriate Intelligence Community partners.

(S) The ELINT Parameter Limits (EPL) details the radar characteristics of many U.S. and allied weapon systems, including most of those in use by Taiwan. For most emitters in use by potential PRC adversaries, the PRC likely already has collected most of this information. Potential foreign partner impact from the loss of the EPL, therefore, is considered low.

(S) Regarding the EOB, the compromised information could provide the PRC with a good starting point for identifying the total electronic threat posed by a country, but it is information that in all likelihood the PRC already has. Potential foreign partner impact from the loss of the EOB, therefore, is considered low.

6.3.5 (U) Recommendation

- (U) Coordinate notification procedures and notify foreign partners of pertinent information compromised to the PRC.

6.4 (U) PRC Sharing and Previous Access to Compromised Data

TOP SECRET//COMINT//NOFORN//X1

TOP SECRET//COMINT//NOFORN//X1

6.4.1 **(U) Other Potential Recipients of EP-3E Compromised Data**

(C) The PRC's leadership will undoubtedly examine its political and economic objectives and then determine the cost-benefit of sharing the intelligence data with other countries. The PRC, as with all sovereign states, will take steps necessary to safeguard its national security interests. Therefore the information, if shared, will probably be shared on a case-by-case basis.

(S//SI) At a minimum, eight countries bear close scrutiny by the U.S. Cryptologic System and the Intelligence Community. These countries include North Korea, Vietnam, Cuba (all deemed to be fraternal Communist states), Russia, the Ukraine, Iraq, Belarus (which engage in military sales and technology transfer with the PRC), and Pakistan (a strategic partner). Changes in the communications infrastructure of these nations could pose significant challenges for the U.S. Cryptologic System and its ability to support policymakers. This list of countries, while not exhaustive, represents a starting point for community analytic efforts.

6.4.2 **(U) Previous Cryptologic Compromises to the PRC**

(TS//SI//NF) The EP-3E incident was not the first compromise of U.S. tactical cryptologic sources and methods or other sensitive information to the PRC or its closest partners. North Korea's seizure of the USS Pueblo in 1968 and espionage cases in the 1980s and 1990s provided the PRC with insight into the U.S. Cryptologic System's targeting of its tactical and encrypted communications. There are indications that PRC operatives have actively sought to acquire U.S. COMSEC equipments and manuals. Additionally, one of the PRC's closest partners, Russia, has acquired similar information on U.S. targeting of special submarine communications, PROFORMA, and many of the USSIDs that were onboard the EP-3E. Although there is no direct evidence that Russia has shared any of this information with the PRC, the PRC has probably benefited from information gleaned from previously compromised equipment.

(S//SI) The impact of these past compromises on U.S. intelligence efforts has been mixed. In some instances, targeted communications have disappeared, i.e., either ceased transmitting or migrated to other modes of communications, and in others there were no target changes at all. Regardless of detected target changes, previous compromises have heightened the PRC's awareness of its communications vulnerabilities and increased the probability of the U.S. facing a constantly evolving and more sophisticated PRC communications target.

6.5 **(U) Counterintelligence Issues**

TOP SECRET//COMINT//NOFORN//X1

TOP SECRET//COMINT//NOFORN//X1

6.5.1 (U) Findings

- (C) Names and organizations of Intelligence Community and foreign partner personnel were disclosed in documentation onboard the EP-3E.
- (C) Much of the information regarding individual identities was contained in the forwarding instructions for NSA's tasking database and in the MARTES source code.
- (C) A substantial amount of personnel data unnecessary for the mission was onboard.
- (C) Initial inspection of the recovered aircraft at Dobbins Air Reserve Base in Marietta, Georgia, found no evidence of PRC implants.
- (S) No cryptologic information was compromised as a result of the PRC's interrogation of the EP-3E crew.

6.5.2 (U) Compromise of Personnel

(S//SI) As a result of the incident, individual identities and their affiliations with U.S. intelligence operations were revealed to the PRC. Most names were located in SIGINT documentation or software, including several dozen individuals identified as employees of NSA and NSGA Misawa.

(C) Additionally, extensive personnel information was carried onboard by the crew. Names, addresses, social security numbers and official duties of crew members and personnel not on the aircraft were disclosed on travel orders and other documents.

(U//FOUO) The NSA Office of Security has contacted all individuals to discuss these counterintelligence concerns. For some personnel, future assignments and travel may be adversely affected.

6.5.3 (U) Inspection of Recovered Aircraft

(C) Experts in counterintelligence and reverse engineering inspected the returned aircraft and its contents for equipment tampering and evidence of reverse engineering. No evidence was found of PRC implants or bugging devices, although it is possible that an implant could have been undetectable. There were signs of PRC intrusion into many pieces of equipment that could indicate PRC attempts at reverse engineering.

(S) The team conducted extensive searches of the interior of the aircraft. These searches recovered a laptop computer hard drive and several fragments of cryptographic key, cassette tape, and classified paper documents. During the search process, the team removed floorboards, insulation and all soft panels, and used borescopes to inspect areas beyond physical access. Further analysis of component parts continues.

(S) In all, the team removed and examined over 500 pieces of equipment from the aircraft and inspected roughly 300 items for evidence of tampering. In some cases, the

TOP SECRET//COMINT//NOFORN//X1

TOP SECRET//COMINT//NOFORN//X1

PRC made little or no effort to conceal its inspection efforts, replacing equipment with obvious indications that it had been removed and examined (e.g., one piece was mounted upside down, some equipment was not secured with screws, connectors were not reattached). In other cases, the PRC's efforts to reverse engineer some computer boards and chips were detectable only with a microscope.

6.5.4 (U) PRC Interaction with the Crew

(C) The crew did not reveal any cryptologic information during its 11-day detention. PRC personnel interacted daily with the crew and questioned crew members regarding their duties and their mission. Responses from the crew, no matter how unbelievable or mundane, were not challenged, and PRC personnel did not pressure the crew to provide information beyond what was offered. Questioning focused on the incident, and PRC personnel attempted to gain admissions of guilt or remorse for the collision. Secondarily, the PRC personnel used the sessions to make political statements regarding the humane nature of the treatment provided and the peaceful wishes of the PRC. These statements were often cited in conjunction with alleged "crimes" that the EP-3E had committed, such as causing the collision, violating PRC airspace, landing without permission, and spying. The PRC personnel also used the sessions as an opportunity to lecture crew members on PRC and world history. None of the crew expressed the view that they felt obligated or intimidated to provide information.

(U//FOUO) A detailed report on the crew's activities and experiences during is being prepared by the Joint Personnel Recovery Agency.

6.5.5 (U) Recommendations

- (U//FOUO) Remove names of all individuals and organizations from forwarding instructions, technical material, and software carried on SRO or other sensitive SIGINT operations.
- (U//FOUO) Reduce the amount of personnel information in mission materials to the minimum possible. Do not reference organizations, offices, or names of personnel.

6.6 (U) Potential for Recovery of Jettisoned Equipment

(S) There is a very low probability that the PRC would be able to recover items jettisoned from the EP-3E. Jettisoning took place over a wide area as the aircraft flew toward Hainan Island, and consisted of physically small objects. Jettisoned items were limited to COMSEC and ELINT materials, including a metal box with COMSEC keying material and codebooks, some COMSEC electronic fill devices, and two ELINT laptop computers. There is no evidence that the PRC observed the jettisoning of materials.

(S//NF) The most reliable way to locate small, widely dispersed objects on the seafloor is through use of a side-scan sonar search system. The PRC has access to these

TOP SECRET//COMINT//NOFORN//X1

systems, but the large search area, bottom topography, and small size of the objects makes location and recovery of any material very unlikely.

(S//NF) There have been no indications of any PRC recovery efforts other than initial search and recovery attempts focusing on the F-8 II and its pilot. The Office of Naval Intelligence is monitoring the area for signs of recovery activity, but limited U.S. collection assets in the region mean that it is possible that the PRC could conduct such a search without being detected.

TOP SECRET//COMINT//NOFORN//X1

7.0 (U) U.S. Cryptologic System Crisis Response

7.1 (U) Key Findings

- (C) The EP-3E incident was multifaceted (e.g., military operational, diplomatic, intelligence compromise) but data flow beyond the normal military audience was initially limited.
- (C) Restrictions on dissemination of "raw" SIGINT led to frustration and misunderstanding among some customers.

7.1.1 (U) Introduction

(U) This section reviews the crisis response activities of the U.S. Cryptologic System from the EP-3E collision through repatriation of the crew. It is based on interviews with officials from NSA, JCS, OSD, USCINCPAC, CIA, State, ONI, KRSOC, and the White House (see Appendix H for a complete list). The interviews revealed what worked well during the crisis, what did not work well, and areas for improvement. The findings are separated into eight areas: intelligence support, IA crisis response, crisis management, communications and interagency coordination, SIGINT policy issues, customer views, the crew debriefing process, and damage assessment procedures.

7.1.2 (U) Findings

- (S//SI) SIGINT support to the EP-3E via NICKELBACK advisory support procedures was good.
- (C) The initial CRITIC series reporting the known facts of the collision met timeliness requirements.
- (C) Within hours of the incident, the IA system moved to supersede all keying materials.
- (C) International distress frequencies were not tasked for SIGINT collection during reconnaissance missions.
- (C) At the time of the event, there was no record or playback capability for the Pacific Tributary Network (PTN).
- (U//FOUO) NSA lacks the ability to immediately surge all available SIGINT collection assets.
- (U//FOUO) Customers generally gave SIGINT support good marks.
- (U//FOUO) Interagency communications and coordination worked well.
- (U//FOUO) There was no extant guidance for how to conduct intelligence debriefings as part of JPRA's personnel recovery procedures.
- (U/FOUO) The crew's pre-Easter release and subsequent 30-day leave period did not allow for a timely and comprehensive debriefing.
- (U/FOUO) The cryptologic assessment team was not established until 26 days after the incident.
- (U/FOUO) There were no guidance documents or directives for conducting an intelligence compromise damage assessment.

TOP SECRET//COMINT//NOFORN//X1

- (U//FOUO) In general, operating forces and field activities were more web-enabled than national-level agencies and customers.

7.2 (U) SIGINT Support

(S//SI) Overall, SIGINT support to the EP-3E mission was good. The EP-3E flew under NICKELBACK advisory procedures and was promptly notified by KRSOC of the PRC's initial tracking activities. Until the mission landed at Lingshui, advisory conditions were issued in accordance with procedures.

(S//SI) The CRITIC reporting process worked as designed, delivering the initial information on the EP-3E situation to customers worldwide and to the extended U.S. Cryptologic System. The National Security Operations Center (NSOC) orchestrated the dissemination and coordination of the CRITIC reporting series and convened a conference of senior intelligence officers at the White House, the Pentagon, the State Department, and CIA. This conferencing system, known as a NOIWON, enabled senior personnel to discuss and coordinate events throughout the early stages of the crisis.

(S//SI) The Pacific Tributary Network (PTN) played a key role in providing initial insight into the unfolding crisis. NSOC's Special Support Activity (SSA), KRSOC, as well as PACROC monitored the initial maydays via the PTN. During the crisis, watch centers monitored these live communications without any capability to record and retrieve them. Although this could have potentially caused problems in verifying events, it did not become an issue. Record and playback capabilities have since been installed on the SSA's PTN system.

(S//SI) NSA's ability to know at any specific time the totality of overall collection against a specific target is fragmented. In a crisis response situation, the result is that typically 24 hours or more can pass before there is an accurate accounting of all national and tactical systems arrayed against a target. Although NSA immediately began to augment or "surge" collection by working with the Intelligence Community to steer systems such as overhead satellites to increase coverage of the PRC, other collection assets were not tasked as rapidly. Such a delay can result in important collection opportunities being forfeited in the early, and perhaps most important, stages of a crisis.

(S//SI) NSA's lack of collection of the EP-3E's MAYDAYs was also cited by some as an issue. NSA assets collected one broadcast minutes before the EP-3E landed at Lingshui, but only because of the re-tasking of an overhead satellite in response to the CRITIC. Many customers were unaware that the U.S. Cryptologic System does not routinely monitor international distress frequencies during SRO missions due to resource constraints and competing priorities for other collection.

7.3 (U) IA Crisis Response

(S) Crisis procedures for NSA's Information Assurance Directorate (IAD) worked well. IAD headquarters personnel contacted representatives in Okinawa for assistance in identifying the EP-3E's COMSEC materials and equipments, and a message was sent to the appropriate Controlling Authorities on 1 April instructing the supersession of all affected COMSEC material. IAD personnel ensured that all required keying material was available in theater or could be expeditiously produced and distributed. Over-the-air-transfer of keying materials was accomplished where possible. Additionally, NSA's Joint COMSEC Monitoring Activity provided monitoring support to CINCPAC, CINCPACFLT, and COMSEVENTHFLT during the entire event.

7.4 (U) Crisis Management

(S) NSA's National Security Operations Center (NSOC) served as the central clearinghouse for all EP-3E information with the Senior Operations Officer (SOO) handling requests from Defense, CIA, State, and White House officials. After two days, however, the deluge of calls began to impact the SOO's other duties. This led to a decision to establish an EP-3 desk to serve as the focal point for all EP-3E related matters. The EP-3 desk stood up officially on Tuesday, 3 April. Most customers praised NSOC's responsiveness and its twice-daily SIGINT updates. Although the EP-3 desk performed well, customer inquiries eventually consumed most of the desk officers' time. Some customers sought an EP-3 website where they could go for related data, but such a site was not established during this crisis. Crisis-related websites at JICPAC and KRSOC were praised for their usefulness. In general, the operating forces and field activities are more web-active than national-level organizations.

(U//FOUO) Crisis management procedures are under review in the Defense Department, specifically focusing on the roles, functions, and interaction of the numerous watch centers throughout the Pentagon. Similarly, NSA is studying how to optimize its new organizational structure for crisis management. Improvements not withstanding, the current structure provided effective crisis support during the incident.

7.5 (U) Communications and Interagency Coordination

(S) Communications worked well throughout the incident. A number of those interviewed cited the State Department-chaired, daily video teleconferences as an excellent way to coordinate and share information. Similarly, watch officers cited "ZIRCON chat" –essentially an on-going secure chat room available over the Joint Worldwide Intelligence Communications System secure network– as an effective method for communicating and sharing information. A limitation inherent in this type of communication, though, is that information in the chat room is not authoritative and may be misleading.

(S) Interagency coordination involving the sharing of EP-3E operational information was described by several parties as problematic. Operational information that would have been useful outside of military channels was not disseminated. Non-military customers cite the fact that the EP-3E incident was more than just a military operational issue; it was also a political, diplomatic, and intelligence issue. In particular, data sharing by military components during an incident such as this could have, and should have, been more robust.

7.6 (U) SIGINT Policy Issues

(S//SI) During the incident, a number of customers asked to see the transcript of the conversation between the PRC fighter intercept controller and the surviving PRC F-8-II pilot. This transcript, defined by NSA as "raw" SIGINT, had served as the basis for a SIGINT product report already issued. Current NSA policy allows for release of raw SIGINT to customers, in accordance with written procedures.

(C) Uncertainty by NSA officials over whether or not to release the raw SIGINT ultimately led to a request for guidance from the Secretary of Defense on how NSA should handle the requests for this information. The guidance provided was to limit sharing of this information to select senior officials at the Pentagon and CIA, and only under strict handling procedures. Initially, the list did not include the JCS J2, State Department officials, or members of congressional oversight committees, though the Deputy Secretary of State and JCS J2 were added later. The Chairman of the House Permanent Select Committee on Intelligence, who had specifically requested the transcript, was not added. These actions frustrated customers and oversight officials, and fostered a perception that NSA was holding back key intelligence.

(C) NSA's Signals Intelligence Directorate is reviewing and revising its policy on raw SIGINT. This review was underway prior to the EP-3E incident. The EP-3E incident highlighted misunderstandings within the U.S. Cryptologic System regarding providing raw SIGINT to customers. For example, some managers had a false impression that the requests for raw SIGINT required legal review when in fact it is a policy, not a legal issue. Also, NSA officers in the field differed in their interpretations of their responsibilities to handle raw SIGINT.

7.7 (U) Customer Views

(S//SI) Generally, SIGINT reporting during the incident received high marks. Specifically, the ADCI for Collection praised NSA's efforts against the PRC leadership target during negotiations for the EP-3E's crew release. Also, the CRITIC reporting series was valuable to customers.

(S//SI) Customer expectations during a crisis such as this are subject to change, usually without notice. Immediately following the collision, many customers adjusted their information threshold. Data previously deemed insignificant, e.g., routine PRC transport flights in and around Lingshui airfield, quickly became unique and critical to many customers. During this crisis customers expected to be informed of what the U.S. Cryptologic System knew, what it did not know, and any additional insight, even that which would not be reported. This was deemed critical by Intelligence Community analysts for policymaker support.

TOP SECRET//COMINT//NOFORN//X1

7.8 (U) Crew Debriefing Procedures

(S) The Joint Personnel Recovery Agency (JPRA), part of the Joint Forces Command, is the lead organization chartered with the safe and efficient repatriation of U.S. military personnel, and in some cases, U.S. civilians and other individuals. JPRA conducted non-intelligence related debriefings of the crew and advised and trained the intelligence debriefing teams.

(S) Following their 11-day detention, the repatriated crew was immediately made available for JPRA and intelligence debriefings in Hawaii. Six three-person debriefing teams were formed to debrief the 24 crew members regarding intelligence loss and compromise. Each team consisted of a representative from either the Defense HUMINT Service or Naval Criminal Investigative Service, a Navy representative with EP-3E flight experience, and an NSA subject matter expert.

(S) The CINCPACFLT Director of Intelligence (N2) and Director for Cryptology (N3DC) were responsible for forming the intelligence debriefing teams and developing the methodology and questions required to assess the potential intelligence loss from this incident. CINCPACFLT N2 prepared a CONOP without benefit of written guidelines.

(S) The time allotted for the initial debriefings was too short and the period between the initial intelligence debriefings and follow-up re-interviews was too long. JPRA guidance recommended at least 72 hours to complete both the JPRA and intelligence debriefs. Due to the decision to release the crew for the Easter holiday, this time was reduced to 42 hours. Furthermore, the crew was not available for follow-up debriefings for over 30 days. During this time, the crew's recall of events was affected by numerous events and interactions. By the time of their Maryland re-interviews, accuracy of the individual accounts of events had degraded. While we assess that in this case the overall accuracy of our findings was not impacted, it easily could have been had the PRC not returned certain equipments (e.g., the MARTES laptop and SCARAB computer). In order to increase the accuracy of future damage assessments, the intelligence debriefing process must be allowed sufficient time and be completed as soon as possible after such a compromise.

7.9 (U) Damage Assessment Procedures

(S) Although the potential damage to U.S. intelligence capabilities was an issue from the outset, the EP-3 Cryptologic Assessment Team was not established until 26 days after the incident. In hindsight, it should have been formed immediately. The team did not identify any guidance documents or directives for conducting an intelligence compromise damage assessment.

7.10 (U) Recommendations

- (U//FOUO) Implement streamlined NSA policy regarding raw SIGINT.

TOP SECRET//COMINT//NOFORN//X1

TOP SECRET//COMINT//NOFORN//X1

- (U//FOUO) The Secretary of Defense in coordination with the DCI should charter a damage assessment team within 48 hours of a potential intelligence compromise involving DoD assets. The team should serve as the lead for producing findings, the damage assessment, and recommendations.
- (U//FOUO) Implement procedures to increase the SIGINT system's responsiveness during crisis events.
- (C) Tie the monitoring of international distress frequencies to specific NICKELBACK advisory conditions.
- (U//FOUO) Acquire a record and playback capability immediately for all Pacific Tributary Network (PTN) broadcasts at the KRSOC.
- (U//FOUO) Allot sufficient time for intelligence debriefings in order to allow a thorough determination of potentially compromised data.
- (U//FOUO) Incorporate intelligence debriefing into JPRA personnel recovery procedures if there is an Intelligence Community equity.
- (U//FOUO) The Secretary of Defense and the DCI jointly prepare a damage assessment "how to" guide for intelligence compromises.

TOP SECRET//COMINT//NOFORN//X1

8.0 (U) Emergency Processes and Procedures

8.1 (U) Key Findings

- (U//FOUO) No specific guidance existed regarding Mission Commander or aircrew actions should an SRO aircraft be forced or, through emergency, be required to land in the PRC.
- (C) A substantial amount of non-mission-essential classified information was carried onboard the aircraft.
- (C) Inventory procedures did not require sufficient detail to identify reliably the content of classified equipments, computers, or hardcopy materials.
- (C) Crew training for emergency destruction was minimal and did not meet squadron requirements; this deficiency was the primary cause of the compromise of classified material.
- (C) There was sufficient time to jettison all sensitive materials from the aircraft.

8.1.1 (U) Introduction

(U) This section reviews emergency processes and procedures that applied to the EP-3E mission. It reviews policy, radio communications, internal communications, classification and material handling, emergency destruction policy, procedures, and training, and crew reaction. It also includes a discussion of procedures employed by other tactical SIGINT platforms. For reference, a schematic of the EP-3E with position identifications is included in Appendix F.

8.2 (U) Policy

8.2.1 (U) Findings

- (U//FOUO) There was no policy guidance regarding actions to be taken in the event of hazardous maneuvers by reacting PRC fighter aircraft.
- (U//FOUO) Faced with hazardous PRC fighter maneuvers, several of the crew remained out of their seats.
- (C) The Mission Commander, although in communication with the Pacific Reconnaissance Operations Center after landing at Lingshui Airfield, did not request instructions or guidance from higher authority.
- (U//FOUO) Peacetime detention training was optional for Navy aircrew; nine of the EP-3E crew members had not received the training.

8.2.2 (U) Discussion

(S) PRC fighter reactions to SRO missions in the South China Sea, specifically those by Lingshui-based fighters, had become increasingly aggressive in the months preceding the collision incident. Reacting aircraft frequently approached to within 100 feet of the mission aircraft, and on four occasions, within 50 feet. The closest previous

TOP SECRET//COMINT//NOFORN//X1

approach was within ten feet. The U.S. government was aware of the potential hazards imposed by such activity and delivered a demarche on the topic to Beijing in December 2000. However, neither the Pacific Command nor the JCS issued any new guidance regarding actions to be taken in the event of close encounters by reacting PRC fighter aircraft. At the time of the collision, several crew members were out of their seats. Though crew members were not injured, they could have been and this could have made a difficult situation far worse.

(S) SRO flight crews operating in the Pacific theater lacked specific guidance on divert airfields under emergency conditions. There were no written policies or procedures that specified countries to which the aircraft could or could not divert under emergency situations, crew actions to be taken in the event of emergency diverts, contingency statements for crew use, specific instructions regarding disposition of materials, or whether or not the aircraft should be destroyed, and if so, how.

(S) After the collision, the Mission Commander assessed his ability to fly the aircraft, the airworthiness of the aircraft, and the options available (i.e., bailout, ditch, land). The Mission Commander elected to divert to the closest airfield, at Lingshui on Hainan Island. Once the aircraft had landed, a cadre of PRC military, some of whom were armed with bolt-action rifles, almost immediately surrounded it, though none aimed weapons at the aircraft. Based on his assessment of growing PRC impatience, the Mission Commander ordered the plane powered down, thereby terminating communications with the Pacific Reconnaissance Operations Center, and ordered the crew to deplane.

(S) The PRC detained the crew for 11 days. Nine of the crew, including the Mission Commander, had not received peacetime detention training. This training addresses the legal rights and responsibilities of aircrews facing precisely the circumstances this crew encountered and provides methods and techniques for dealing with detention, interrogation, and isolation. A review of the crew's detention experience is contained in a separate report issued by the Joint Personnel Recovery Agency.

(S) A bilateral agreement with Russia establishes procedures for the peaceful handling and expeditious resolution of similar incidents between U.S. and Russian forces. *The Agreement Between the United States and Russia on the Prevention of Dangerous Military Activities* specifies procedures for both parties in the event of distress (*force majeure*) entry of U.S. forces into Russian territory. U.S. aircrews (including the incident EP-3E crew) carry specific guidance in their Flight Information Handbook covering the implementation of this agreement. This guidance includes frequencies, call signs, standard phraseology and a Russian language checklist for use after landing. No similar agreement exists between the U.S. and the PRC.

8.2.3 (U) Recommendations

TOP SECRET//COMINT//NOFORN//X1

- (C) Establish written guidance for aircrew actions in the event of hazardous maneuvers by reacting fighters.
- (C) Provide detailed guidance for Mission Commander and crew actions in the event of a forced landing of the mission aircraft in countries within range of the mission track.
- (U//FOUO) Require peacetime detention training for all reconnaissance personnel and personnel engaged in other sensitive operations where there is a risk of detention.
- (U//FOUO) Explore pursuing an agreement with the PRC to establish joint procedures to prevent dangerous military activities.

8.3 (U) Radio Communications

8.3.1 (U) Findings

- (C) The flight crew defaulted to U.S. military emergency communications procedures that were ineffective in establishing contact with the PRC.
- (C) The flight crew was unfamiliar with PRC aeronautical frequency usage and did not attempt contact with Lingshui on local airfield frequencies.
- (C) Emergency destruction efforts directed at communications equipment placed the aircrew out of radio contact until after landing. At that time, the aircrew briefly restored secure communications with PACROC until terminating connectivity prior to deplaning.

8.3.2 (U) Radio Equipment and Networks

(U//FOUO) The EP-3E has numerous radios onboard and is a participant on a wide variety of radio networks. Line-of-sight communications are conducted using both plain voice and secure VHF and UHF radios. On SRO missions, long-range communications with controlling authorities are conducted via HF radio and over a number of secure UHF satellite networks. For a listing of EP-3E radio equipment and networks, see Appendix E.

8.3.3 (U) Emergency Communications

(U) United States and allied military aviation communications take place almost entirely within the frequency band from 225.0 MHz to 399.9 MHz. U.S. military pilots receive the majority of their training in this band, including the use of the 243.0 MHz emergency frequency. EP-3E flight station radios have an emergency setting that tunes directly to 243.0 MHz.

(C) DoD Flight Information Publications carried onboard the EP-3E list several international emergency frequencies, including both 121.5 MHz and 243.0 MHz, and state in general that any may be used. No guidance is provided specific to emergency contact with the PRC.

TOP SECRET//COMINT//NOFORN//X1

TOP SECRET//COMINT//NOFORN//X1

8.3.4 **(U) Procedures Used During Incident**

(S) At the time of the incident, secure communications via satellite had been established with KRSOC and the Special Support Activity (SSA) in NSOC on the Pacific Tributary Network (PTN), and with KRSOC on the SENSOR PACER network. HF reception and connectivity using the Global High Frequency System (GHFS) was poor.

(S) In the first moments after the collision, the secure communications operator attempted repeatedly to transmit the two-word message "GOING DOWN" on the SENSOR PACER network. This message was never received. Further transmissions were precluded by the emergency destruction of secure communications equipment.

(S) The navigator transmitted MAYDAY calls on PTN. At least one transmission was received by both KRSOC and SSA, initiating CRITIC reporting. The navigator also transmitted MAYDAY calls on the GHFS frequency of 13200 kHz. These calls were never received.

(S//SI) The aircrew transmitted repeated MAYDAY calls on the UHF emergency frequency 243.0 MHz. At no time did the aircrew transmit on the VHF emergency frequency of 121.5 MHz or any frequency associated with Lingshui Airfield. Training of flight station personnel did not address either the PRC usage of the VHF band for military aircraft communications or PRC emergency communications procedures. Efforts to locate Lingshui Airfield frequencies in DoD flight information publications were unsuccessful, since PRC military airfields are not listed. COMINT operators on the aircraft were familiar with the Lingshui Airfield frequency (128.5 MHz) and PRC-wide military aviation frequencies (126.0 and 130.0 MHz), but the flight station did not engage the COMINT operators on this issue.

(S) Power was removed from the PTN satellite voice radio during the emergency destruction process, erasing all frequencies from the radio's memory. Although the crew destroyed the radio's cryptographic keying material and PTN frequency documentation, it did not zeroize the radio's encryption device.

(S) After landing, the SEVAL was able to recall the PTN frequency and retune the radio, enabling the crew to re-establish secure two-way communications with the Pacific Reconnaissance Operations Center (PACROC), KRSOC, and Special Support Activity (SSA). The crew then transmitted the final message from the aircraft before zeroizing the PTN radio's encryption device.

8.3.5 **(U) Recommendations**

TOP SECRET//COMINT//NOFORN//X1

TOP SECRET//COMINT//NOFORN//X1

- (U//FOUO) Incorporate guidance in emergency destruction procedures identifying communication equipment that should not be zeroized or destroyed until no longer needed.
- (U//FOUO) Train flight crew personnel in the emergency communication procedures used by countries in their areas of operations.
- (U//FOUO) Provide guidance in the DoD Flight Information Handbook specific to emergency communications with the PRC and other target nations.

8.4 (U) Internal Communications

8.4.1 (U) Findings

- (C) A breakdown in communications and situational awareness occurred throughout the aircraft immediately following the collision.
- (C) Public address (PA) announcements were nearly unintelligible in the noisy environment after the collision; many crew members reported an inability to clearly understand PA commands once they had donned helmets.
- (C) The inability to effectively communicate orders and intentions contributed significantly to the incomplete destruction effort.
- (C) The decision to land instead of ditching the aircraft was not communicated to the entire crew.

8.4.2 (U) Internal Communication System

(C) The EP-3E's internal communications system is the Digital Communications Management System (DCMS). All operational crew positions have access to the DCMS with headsets, with the exception of personnel in the galley and observers in the flight station. Communication paths between crew members are divided into various audio networks. The primary network is the ALL net (available at all crew stations). An internal PA system, consisting of small loudspeakers distributed throughout the aircraft cabin, is available for internal announcements. PA system announcements override DCMS traffic at every crew station. Helmets can be connected to the DCMS using the same cable that connects headsets. Helmets are tight-fitting and acoustically isolate the wearer from his or her surroundings.

8.4.3 (U) Normal Mission Communications

(S) There is no specific written guidance on DCMS net configuration or employment. During periods of heightened activity, such as when the aircraft is being intercepted, the entire crew usually switches to the ALL net to maximize their situational awareness. In the case of an intercept, this allows all personnel to hear observer reports on the intercepting aircraft. As an exception to this practice, the COMINT operators monitoring target nation communications may deselect the ALL net to minimize distraction and interference.

TOP SECRET//COMINT//NOFORN//X1

TOP SECRET//COMINT//NOFORN//X1

(U//FOUO) During emergencies, the SEVAL serves as the point of contact between the Aircraft Commander in the flight station and the crew, orchestrating the safe completion of emergency procedures. The flight station also communicates to the crew aft using the PA system.

(U//FOUO) It was not a procedural requirement for all EP-3E crew members to monitor DCMS during landings.

8.4.4 (U) Procedures Used During Incident

(S) At the time of the intercept, several crew members were not connected to the DCMS. These included a third pilot and second flight engineer acting as observers in the flight station, a roving photographer, and an ELINT operator trainee. All other crew members were monitoring the ALL net with the exception of COMINT operators engaged in collection.

(C) After the collision, the first command issued by the Mission Commander was to prepare to bail out. This command was issued via the PA. All crew members removed their headsets in order to don their parachutes, survival vests and helmets.

(C) High noise levels resulting from aircraft damage gave crew members wearing helmets great difficulty hearing each other, even when shouting at close range. PA announcements were also difficult to hear. At this point, communication of orders and instructions to the crew became unreliable.

(C) Acting as jumpmaster, the SEVAL connected his helmet to a DCMS interface but was unable to communicate with the flight station due to a failed microphone. Consequently, he sent a runner to the cockpit to inform the Mission Commander that the crew was prepared to bail out.

(C) After issuing the command to prepare to bail out, the Mission Commander regained control of the aircraft, negating the need to bail out. The Mission Commander then issued a PA announcement notifying the crew to prepare to ditch and to commence emergency destruction.

(C) As emergency destruction began, crew members aft of the navigation station did not connect their helmets to the DCMS in order to have free movement for destruction activity. As a result, no one heard flight station discussions on the ALL net concerning landing at Lingshui. Although the Mission Commander did not make a PA announcement regarding the decision to attempt landing at Lingshui, the SEVAL did learn of the intention through face-to-face communication with the Mission Commander. However, he did not communicate this information to the rest of the crew.

(C) Only after strapping themselves in for the expected ditching did some personnel connect their helmets to the DCMS. Some crew members cited difficulty doing so due to tangled cords or unfamiliarity with the helmet DCMS cable connection.

TOP SECRET//COMINT//NOFORN//X1

TOP SECRET//COMINT//NOFORN//X1

Others had taken assigned ditching stations in the galley, and had no DCMS access. As a result, many crew members did not realize the aircraft was landing instead of ditching until they either saw land out a window or heard the landing gear deploy.

8.4.5 (U) Recommendations

- (U//FOUO) Improve the performance and intelligibility of the EP-3E PA system to operate better in all environments.
- (U//FOUO) Increase training using helmets during drills so that crew members are proficient at communicating while wearing helmets.
- (U//FOUO) Reemphasize the critical role of clear communications between the flight station and aircrew cabin during emergency procedure and Aircrew Coordination Training.
- (U//FOUO) Drill emergency crew communications procedures in-flight on a routine basis, practicing alternate communication methods for all combinations of emergencies.
- (U//FOUO) As a required part of pre-mission briefings, identify by name key personnel and alternates responsible for leading crew actions and making status reports during emergency destruction.
- (U//FOUO) Design and implement improved emergency communications procedures and hardware on the EP-3E to enable reliable communications at all times, especially during abnormal flight conditions. Investigate wireless communications systems.

8.5 (U) Classified and Sensitive Material Handling

8.5.1 (U) Findings

- (C//SI) Standard operating procedures did not restrict the amount of classified information that could be brought onboard the EP-3E.
- (C//SI) The Mission Commander was unaware of and did not specifically approve any Category III COMINT materials carried onboard.
- (C) The inventory left by the mission aircraft prior to departing on the mission was not accurate, detailed, or verified.
- (C) Operational information such as radio call signs and networks was compromised.

8.5.2 (U) Policy Directives

(U//FOUO) Basic guidance for security procedures for COMINT materials for airborne SIGINT platforms is set forth in USSID 3, *Cryptologic Security Procedures*.

(C//SI) USSID 3 details COMINT restrictions for airborne SIGINT platforms. The USSID specifies that material up to and including Category III (Top Secret) COMINT may be brought onboard, but a designee must review the material to determine whether it applies to the specific mission. USSID 3 further requires that ground

TOP SECRET//COMINT//NOFORN//X1

TOP SECRET//COMINT//NOFORN//X1

personnel conduct an inventory of all COMINT material prior to its being placed onboard the platform, and that ground personnel retain a copy of the inventory.

8.5.3 (U) EP-3E Procedures

(C) Standard operating procedures did not restrict the amount of classified information that could be brought onboard the aircraft.

(C) Considerable operator training takes place airborne during missions. Such training is conducted on a not-to-interfere basis, usually during transit to and from the operational area. Material carried onboard to support training included classified publications and individualized study guides containing target nation orders of battle, notes on signal and weapons systems employment, and SIGINT reporting procedures.

(C) Mission classified material inventories contain a list of publications and positional technical working aids by title, individual study guides, electronic media and portable equipments. This inventory does not include a complete listing of files stored on disks or computer hard drives, or detailed information on contents, sources, and extracts contained in the positional working aids.

8.5.4 (U) Pre-flight Procedures

(C) The aircrew produced a classified material inventory and left it with ground support personnel in Okinawa. However, the inventory was incomplete and not of sufficient detail to allow a detailed reconstruction of materials carried onboard. Some classified materials were not known to have been onboard until the aircraft was recovered.

(C) The aircrew did not limit classified material to that necessary for the conduct of the mission. Technical working aids contained material covering Russia, North Korea, India, and the Persian Gulf, as well as intelligence on the PRC not relevant to the mission. Additionally, the crew carried substantial training materials and study aids not required for the mission.

(C) Portable computers contained extensive classified material that was neither inventoried nor necessary for the mission. Some such material was included in classified software distributions, some was loaded for in-flight reference, and some was unintentionally and unknowingly loaded onto hard drives. Still more material had been generated during or in support of previous missions, but not removed. For material that had been removed but was not overwritten, recoverable fragments of deleted files likely remained. In most cases, the detail and scope of classified material stored on portable computers was unknown to both the aircrew and ground support personnel.

(C) Personnel most responsible for classified material handling had an insufficient understanding of their responsibilities. In particular, the Mission Commander, SEVAL, and COMEVAL had incomplete knowledge of the nature, content and amount of

TOP SECRET//COMINT//NOFORN//X1

TOP SECRET//COMINT//NOFORN//X1

classified material on the aircraft. Additionally, individual operators were not knowledgeable of the scope and contents of files contained on electronic media, or the detailed contents of study guides.

8.5.5 (U) Compromised Operational Information

(C) Several radio call signs and networks and other operational information were compromised by documentation left onboard the aircraft. Information included network names, employment, frequencies; cryptographic keying material assignments; and SRO track coordinates. Damage from this compromise is low.

(C) Additionally, extensive personnel information was carried onboard by the crew (see Section 6.5, Counterintelligence Issues).

8.5.6 (U) Recommendations

- (C) Ensure the Mission Commander and other personnel responsible for emergency destruction are fully cognizant of the scope and nature of all classified materials onboard the aircraft and are in compliance with USSID 3.
- (C) Review USSID 3 requirements for the protection of COMINT systems and data at all classification levels.
- (U//FOUO) Issue policy to increase the detail in material inventories to support a rapid and accurate page-for-page reconstruction of all sensitive and classified materials, including all files on hard disks, CD ROMs, and floppy disks.
- (U//FOUO) Maintain exact backup copies of all electronic media at a ground support facility for every mission.
- (U/FOUO) Establish written procedures designating specific ground support personnel who will verify aircraft inventories and electronic media backups prior to every mission.
- (C) Review and change, as required, compromised operational information such as radio call signs and frequencies.

8.6 (U) Emergency Destruction Policy, Procedures, and Training

8.6.1 (U) Findings

- (C) No specific guidance regarding emergency destruction techniques was provided by SSO Navy or NSA.
- (C) An inventory of destroyed materials and equipments was not kept.

8.6.2 (U) Policy

(U//FOUO) Basic policy for emergency destruction of cryptologic materials is set forth in USSID 3, *Cryptologic Security Procedures*, USSID 702, *Automated Information Systems Security*, NSA/CSS Manual 130-2, *Media Declassification and Destruction*

TOP SECRET//COMINT//NOFORN//X1

Manual, and DCID 1/21, *Physical Security Standards for Sensitive Compartmented Information Facilities.*

(C//SI) USSID 3 states that any emergency destruction that renders classified material and systems unusable is sufficient, but provides no guidance regarding suitable techniques. USSID 702 promulgates NSA/CSS Manual 130-2, which provides a thorough and technical discussion of procedures for the routine sanitization and declassification of electronic media and for its end-of-life destruction, but does not identify suitable emergency procedures. DCID 1/21 establishes security standards for sensitive compartmented information (SCI). For aircraft, the DCID states that if a landing in unfriendly territory is anticipated, all SCI material will immediately be destroyed, but does not specify procedures or techniques. DCID 1/21 mandates emergency destruction rehearsal, but conditions requiring such rehearsal are ambiguous.

(U//FOUO) Although various Navy directives mandate the existence of emergency action plans, no current Navy directive or publication provides guidance specific to the implementation of emergency destruction procedures.

(C) There is no unifying concept underlying any of the guidance regarding emergency destruction. This issue is discussed in detail in Section 4.4, SIGINT Configuration and Materials Management.

8.6.3 (U) EP-3E Procedures and Training

(C) Squadron requirements and procedures for emergency destruction are set forth in the instruction *VQ-1 Command Emergency Action Plan (EAP)*. This official directive requires emergency destruction to take place if an aircraft is to land in hostile territory or ditch in less than 6000 feet of water. If the aircraft is expected to ditch in more than 6000 feet of water, all classified materials should be permitted to go down with the aircraft.

(C) The instruction details duties for individual crew members. A separate checklist page, intended to be detached and referenced during emergency destruction, is included for each affected crew member. Other than shredding, tearing, jettisoning and striking with an axe, no destruction techniques are specified.

(U//FOUO) Final responsibility for emergency destruction lies with the Mission Commander. The instruction explicitly caveats that emergency destruction is secondary to aircrew safety.

(U//FOUO) The squadron emergency action plan specifies that all squadron personnel receive emergency action plan training. Aircrews are required to incorporate emergency destruction plans and practice drills into predeployment workups and to conduct an emergency destruction drill at least once while deployed.

(U//FOUO) VQ-1 crews and NSG COMINT operators train separately. Predeployment workups and training for VQ-1 take place in the United States, while NSG COMINT operators train in Japan.

(C) At the time of the incident, the EP-3E was not equipped with shredders or other destruction tools. The aircraft's fire axe, a dull hatchet approximately 16 inches long intended for cutting through bulkheads in an emergency evacuation, was used in destruction attempts.

8.6.4 (U) Procedures Used During Incident

(C) Emergency destruction training for the aircrew was minimal. Only one crew member reported ever having participated in an in-flight emergency destruction drill. Fifteen reported having been exposed to emergency destruction procedures in the course of their training without the benefit of drills or walk-throughs. Eight reported no training whatsoever. None had trained for emergency destruction in conjunction with any aircraft emergency. A review of crew training records revealed no documentation other than individual JQR signatures of any emergency destruction training or drills. Training was lackadaisical, with the aircrew generally unengaged and going through the motions using unrealistic scenarios.

(C) The squadron emergency action plan, including crew checklists, was carried onboard the aircraft, but not consulted during the incident. Emergency destruction efforts that took place did not resemble prescribed procedures.

(C) Emergency destruction procedures did not begin until several minutes after the collision. The crew initially focused on preparing to bail out. Only after regaining control of the aircraft did the pilot instruct the crew to prepare to ditch and commence emergency destruction. Many crew members did not hear the PA announcement, but began emergency destruction based on the actions of others around them.

(C) At this point, no crew member aft of the navigation station was connected to the DCMS, so no one person was in a position to oversee and coordinate emergency destruction. As a result, crew activities divided themselves into three independent areas of action: the flight station, including the secure communications operator and navigator; the ELINT operators, including the SEVAL; and the COMINT operators, including the COMEVAL.

(C) The pilots, flight engineers, and navigator were immersed in recovering and maintaining control of the aircraft. Classified and unclassified documents were hurriedly grabbed and passed aft for destruction in an uncoordinated fashion, resulting in the pilots' emergency checklists being removed and destroyed. The navigator gathered some classified documentation and most cryptographic material into the CMS box before it was taken from her and used to batter equipment. Off-duty flight station personnel, believing that ditching was imminent, proceeded to their ditching stations in the galley and did not participate in emergency destruction in any significant way.

TOP SECRET//COMINT//NOFORN//X1

(C) ELINT personnel were unfamiliar with emergency destruction procedures, but proceeded using their best judgment. Operators packed classified material into satchels in preparation for jettisoning, zeroized installed ELINT equipment and computer systems, and physically battered exposed equipment.

(C) The aircraft's fire axe was aggressively employed in attempts to destroy the three ELINT laptop computers. This technique is estimated to have been effective in destroying the hard drive of one laptop, but the other two laptop hard drives are assessed to have survived destruction attempts due in part to operator unfamiliarity with how best to destroy them. Two of the three laptops, including the destroyed laptop, were eventually jettisoned.

(C) Operators also attempted destruction of installed ELINT equipment. Without guidance on how to proceed, they directed the bulk of their efforts toward the relatively fragile displays and controls most accessible at their consoles. While many such units were damaged beyond usability, critical system components such as tuners and signal processors went unscathed due to their rugged construction and relative inaccessibility. Improvised destruction tools included the aluminum CMS box, which sprung open and scattered cryptographic material while being used to smash equipment. Time was wasted gathering and repacking this material.

(C) Jettisoning took place through the starboard overwing hatch. After the hatch was opened, the SEVAL threw materials from the aircraft as three crew members restrained him from being sucked through the opening. Some ELINT documentation, two of the three ELINT laptops, magnetic data tapes, and miscellaneous materials such as binders and keyboards were jettisoned before the hatch was closed. The CMS box containing cryptographic keying material and miscellaneous classified documents was also jettisoned. The crew was unable to maintain an inventory of jettisoned materials.

(C//SI) COMINT personnel were also unfamiliar with emergency destruction procedures. Operators gathered classified documents and passed them forward toward the area of the starboard overwing hatch. At the COMINT Supervisor's station, materials were packed into locking leather satchels for jettisoning, but then stored in a nearby cabinet in anticipation of ditching.

(C//SI) COMINT portable computers were damaged to varying degrees. The COMINT Supervisor's laptop computer (Figure 4) was struck with an axe. The SCARAB computer was thrown to the deck in an unsuccessful attempt to damage the locked-in hard drive. The MARTES laptop was stowed undamaged in the galley in anticipation of ditching.

(C) As the aircraft approached land, the Mission Commander instructed the crew to take their seats and strap in, effectively ending destruction efforts. After landing, further destruction efforts were limited to tearing loose papers and tapes and scattering the resulting material about the aircraft.

TOP SECRET//COMINT//NOFORN//X1

8.6.5 (U) Recommendations

- (U//FOUO) Train aircrew in emergency destruction procedures in a formal setting prior to their operational deployment.
- (U//FOUO) Include emergency destruction classroom training and in-flight drills during crew workups. Include all crew members from all commands participating in operations.
- (U//FOUO) Require regular emergency destruction drills during detachments; include situations where destruction procedures are impeded by simultaneous emergencies (e.g., fire of unknown origin, preparations to bail out and/or ditch) and constrained by time limits.
- (U//FOUO) Include emergency destruction responsibilities and procedures in pre-mission briefings, similar to those for ditching, bailout, and fire of unknown origin.
- (U//FOUO) Issue individualized written emergency destruction procedures in a quick-reference format to all crew members prior to flight.
- (U//FOUO) Include emergency destruction as a sub-area of all positional NATOPS qualifications.
- (U//FOUO) Ensure sufficient type and quantity of emergency destruction tools are onboard mission aircraft.
- (U//FOUO) Develop practical procedures for inventorying jettisoned or destroyed materials.
- (U//FOUO) Conduct and document periodic emergency destruction reviews to ensure procedures are current with technology and mission environment changes.
- (U//FOUO) For any equipment not covered by current emergency destruction procedures, require new procedures and training before allowing the equipment onboard.
- (U//FOUO) Provide national-level guidance for jettisoning classified materials.

8.7 (U) Crew Reaction

8.7.1 (U) Findings

- (C) Individual crew performance during the emergency destruction activities ranged from good to poor.
- (C) Effective communication among three key officers (the Mission Commander, SEVAL and COMEVAL) after the collision would have improved the outcome of emergency destruction.
- (C) A lack of cohesive and unified crew training adversely affected emergency destruction.

TOP SECRET//COMINT//NOFORN//X1

8.7.2 **(U) Discussion**

(C) The aircrew's overall performance in safeguarding classified materials under their charge was poor. Success where it occurred was the result of the common sense focus of a few individuals in an uncoordinated effort and occurred despite a general lack of training, practice in emergency destruction, capabilities, and sound policy.

(C) The crew's efforts should be viewed in light of the severe environmental and human factors they faced. In the aftermath of the collision, every crewmember suffered from some degree of shock. While individual performance can then be expected to suffer, such conditions are not insurmountable. Aggressive, repeated, and thorough training serves to guide the thoughts and actions of personnel in extremis. The crew's execution of often-drilled emergency procedures and preparations to bail out were largely successful. However, a lack of training and practice left the crew unprepared to execute emergency destruction successfully under these adverse conditions.

(C) The SEVAL did not oversee the emergency destruction efforts of the crew as a whole, focusing his attention on the ELINT and COMSEC materials carried onboard by squadron personnel. The proper disposition of COMINT materials and equipments fell to the COMEVAL. Citing time constraints, the SEVAL consciously decided not to retrieve and use the aircraft's copy of the squadron emergency action plan.

(C) The SEVAL personally wielded the fire axe to destroy laptop computers and then jettisoned material through the starboard overwing hatch. By actively engaging in this activity instead of delegating it to other personnel, he isolated himself from knowledge of actions taking place in the rest of the cabin. As a result, he had no situational awareness of the status and scope of emergency destruction and was unable to effectively monitor and direct the actions of the crew.

(C) Although the SEVAL learned of the Mission Commander's intent to attempt to land the aircraft at Lingshui through face-to-face communication, he did not communicate this to the rest of the crew in general or to the COMEVAL in particular.

(C) The COMEVAL did not ascertain or maintain situational awareness of the aircraft's circumstances and Mission Commander's intentions. Assuming that the aircraft was going to ditch, the COMEVAL elected not to jettison classified material. This decision was not coordinated with the SEVAL or the Mission Commander. As a result, the COMEVAL was unsuccessful in meeting the responsibility to ensure destruction of sensitive classified material.

(C) Several personnel, observing COMINT materials being packed and placed in a storage cabinet, were concerned that this material should instead be jettisoned. None took the initiative to assert their concerns to the COMEVAL.

(C) After landing, the COMEVAL did not communicate to the SEVAL or the Mission Commander that all COMINT materials and carry-on equipments were still onboard. Several crew members, also knowing that substantial amounts of classified material remained onboard, similarly failed to raise the issue to their chain of command.

(C) The Mission Commander and SEVAL assumed that emergency destruction efforts were complete. They neither queried the crew to verify the disposition of classified materials nor directed or conducted any form of sweep or search of the aircraft. As he left the aircraft, the Mission Commander assumed that all classified materials had been destroyed or jettisoned and that only scraps of paper and destroyed equipment remained.

(C) The Mission Commander, concerned about the apparent growing impatience of the PRC troops surrounding the aircraft, terminated secure radio communications with PACROC before PACOM authorities could be summoned. He ordered the crew to deplane, placing the crew and the aircraft in PRC control.

(C) During debriefings, many crew members commented on the lack of training as a crew. There was a common view that the coordination and effortlessness that marks outstanding crews is difficult to achieve since training and preparation for the deployment occur separately, the responsibility of two different commands. Frequently, the entire crew for the mission aircraft does not meet as a unit until the first mission of the deployment.

(C) In this case, the crew was not properly organized and trained in preparation for executing emergency destruction of classified material as required by the squadron emergency action plan. Emergency destruction plans and practice drills were not incorporated into aircrew predeployment workups, and no emergency destruction training or drills had been conducted during the deployment.

(C) While required training of the crew would have improved the outcome of this incident, greater crew experience also would have added to the crew's likelihood of success. A few of the enlisted operators had multiple tours and thousands of hours of experience conducting SRO missions. All of the officers in leadership positions were relatively inexperienced (both the Mission Commander and the SEVAL were on their first deployment in these positions) and all were in their first tours conducting SRO missions on this platform. There was one Senior Chief Petty Officer and one First Class Petty Officer onboard. All other enlisted personnel were E5 or junior.

8.7.3 (U) Recommendations

- (U//FOUO) Review and formalize crew certification procedures for each deploying crew. Include demonstrated ability to execute all emergency procedures satisfactorily, and emergency destruction under less than optimal conditions.
- (U//FOUO) As part of individual qualification, require trainees to exercise and demonstrate proper emergency destruction procedures during in-flight examination.

TOP SECRET//COMINT//NOFORN//X1

- (U//FOUO) Examine current organizations with the objective of aligning crew training, cohesion, unity, and overall experience.

8.8 (U) Other Tactical SIGINT Platforms

(U//FOUO) Team members deployed to several locations to gather data on best practices in use on other tactical SIGINT collection platforms. The visits concentrated on gaining insights into procedures for risk management in the day-to-day conduct of tactical intelligence, surveillance and reconnaissance missions. Appendix G contains a complete list of units visited and discussion of procedures used for various platforms.

(U//FOUO) Generally, other tactical SIGINT platforms have processes and procedures similar to the EP-3E, including emergency destruction and training, as well as requirements for control of classified and sensitive equipments and documentation. Assuming the destruction plans are technically appropriate for the materials onboard, crew training and drilling will be the deciding factor in successful emergency destruction.

TOP SECRET//COMINT//NOFORN//X1

9.0 (U) Systemic Issues

9.1 (U) Key Finding

- (C) The incident revealed a systemic complacency regarding policy, planning, and training support to EP-3E SRO missions.

9.2 (U) Discussion

(C) The detailed research, interviews, and data gathering conducted to evaluate this incident have brought the crew's actions, both successful and not, into sharp focus. It is clear that a better-aligned and trained crew could have substantially mitigated, and likely completely avoided, the loss of sensitive material through better communication and more effective action.

(C) Less obvious, but equally as clear, is the systemic complacency of the organizations charged with supporting these Sensitive Reconnaissance Operations. The daily reconnaissance flights conducted by aircrews around the world are the final step in a process that should properly anticipate, plan for, equip, train for, and oversee these operations.

(C) In this case, there was a lack of current guidance regarding a situation that was growing increasingly hazardous. Although the United States had delivered a demarche to the PRC in December 2000 declaring its concern for the actions of the PRC pilots, this concern was not translated by theater- and Washington-level organizations into specific issuance of updated guidance to aircrews.

(S) There was no guidance to the Navy aircrew regarding procedures to be followed should the SRO aircraft be forced by circumstances to land in a target country. In this case, the relatively junior officer in charge of the mission was left to make his best estimate of the correct response. Guidance to crews should be developed and frequently reviewed to ensure the most appropriate response, should a platform be forced to recover in a potentially unfriendly location. Although not a factor in this case, the Navy aircrew was not required to complete peacetime detention training, leaving them less well prepared to deal with the circumstances in which they found themselves.

(C) That the crew was untrained and untested in emergency destruction speaks directly to the process by which the providing commands, in this case VQ-1 and NSGA Misawa, prepared and certified the crew for deployment. Active command oversight of training by experienced, knowledgeable personnel is a prerequisite for success. Review of the procedures by which crews prepare technical materials for onboard support, inventory those materials, and train for their destruction or protection is a fundamental command responsibility. Commander, Naval Security Group Command and the Commanders of Patrol and Reconnaissance Forces should vigorously review and assess these procedures on a regular basis.

(U) It is routine for aircrews to be comprised of personnel from multiple commands, given the range of technical skills and experience needed to successfully meet the complex requirements set for most crews. This places a special burden on providing commands to ensure that crews are trained to the highest state of preparedness. If manning and training cannot be accomplished within the commands' resources (e.g., flight hours available for in-flight emergency destruction training, travel funds for Aircrew Coordination Training), the organizations charged with resourcing those commands must engage and resolve the issue.

(C) Policy for emergency destruction is inadequate and does not account for today's rapidly evolving technologies and the equipments and capabilities being routinely deployed in risky environments. DCI and DIRNSA guidance addresses the requirements for end-state destruction in rigorous detail, but does not address destruction in emergency circumstances, other than to direct that it be accomplished.

(S) New guidance is required that incorporates modern methods of data protection or eradication. Increasingly, our capabilities are not embedded in hardware but reside in software. The U.S. requires a response that changes the paradigm from destruction of equipments and materials to safeguarding information with modern techniques such as encryption and rapid overwriting of hard disks. While destruction may always be preferred, it may not always be possible. Several Intelligence Community organizations are currently working on such applications and have deployed these capabilities on a limited scale. These efforts should be crosswalked, melded into a coherent program, and migrated into operational platforms and missions. This is imperative given that more classified and sensitive capability, not less, will find its way into risky environments where compromise is possible and where destruction is impractical or not possible.

(C) Focused interest and active regard for the protection of classified information should not have to result from substantial, public losses. Complacency is in itself a risk factor. At a time when the intelligence and technical superiority enjoyed by the United States is challenged, we can ill afford to risk this superiority through inattention to the protection of what we do have. The protection of classified information should be on a par with any other emergency procedure that we must be proficient in. This incident has, to this point, energized the Intelligence Community and many actions have already been taken to correct deficiencies. However, follow-through and institutionalization of lessons learned, at all levels, are required to avoid the tendency for loss of focus as incidents recede, memories fade, and emergent issues strain resources. Failure to address these issues decisively will not just continue the likelihood of future losses, it will guarantee it.

9.3 (U) Recommendation

- (U) Implement, track, and institutionalize the study's recommendations.

(U) Glossary

Term	Expansion	Definition/Description
ADCI	Assistant Director of Central Intelligence	n/a
AN/ALD-9	n/a	(U) A direction finder set that calculates the direction of arrival for received HF, VHF, and UHF signals. Installed on the EP-3E.
AN/ALQ-108	n/a	(U) An enemy IFF interrogation system used to actively and passively exploit early Russian IFF and range extension signals. Installed on the EP-3E.
AN/CYZ-10	n/a	(U) The Data Transfer Device currently used in the U.S. Electronic Key Management System.
AN/ULQ-16	n/a	(U) A computerized pulse processor, used to make radar signal measurements. Installed on the EP-3E.
CINCPAC	Commander-in-Chief, Pacific Command	n/a
CINCPACFLT	Commander-in-Chief, Pacific Fleet	n/a
CMS Box	COMSEC Material System Box	(U) A locking metal case used to secure and transport cryptographic codebooks, keying material and cryptographic devices on the EP-3E.
COMEVAL	COMINT Evaluator	(C) The senior COMINT authority aboard Naval reconnaissance aircraft. The COMEVAL supervises COMINT collection and provides interface with the ELINT collection effort for fused reporting.
COMINT	Communications Intelligence	(U) Technical and intelligence information derived from foreign communications by other than intended recipients.
COMINT Supervisor	n/a	(C) An experienced enlisted COMINT operator responsible for monitoring and directing the activities of the COMINT operators on the EP-3.
COMNAVSECGRU	Commander, Naval Security Group	n/a
COMSEC	Communications Security	(U) Technology for securing/protecting voice/data communications
COMSEVENTHFLT	Commander, Seventh Fleet	n/a
CRITIC	Critical Information	(U//FOUO) A report of critical information concerning possible foreign threats to U.S. national security that is so significant that it requires the immediate attention of the President and the National Security Council. CRITICs are delivered within 10 minutes to appropriate intelligence organizations, military components, and other recipients as the DCI may designate.
CTEGM	Collector Technical ELINT Guidance Manual	(C) NSA collection guidance associated with target emitters and systems of technical interest.
DCI	Director of Central Intelligence	n/a
DCID	Director of Central Intelligence Directive	(U) Directives that serve as the principal means by which the DCI provides guidance, policy, and direction to the Intelligence Community.

TOP SECRET//COMINT//NOFORN//X1

Term	Expansion	Definition/Description
DCMS	Digital Communications Management System	(U//FOUO) The EP-3E internal system that provides audio communications between crew members as well as routing of audio signals between transmitters, receivers, navigation instruments and the PA system.
DoD	Department of Defense	n/a
DTD	Data Transfer Device	(U) Fill device designed to securely store, transport, and electronically transfer key.
EDP	Emergency Destruction Procedures	(U) Predefined procedures dealing with the destruction of sensitive material (e.g., computers, documentation, COMSEC keying material).
ELINT	Electronic Intelligence	(U) Technical and intelligence information obtained from the intercept and analysis of non-communication, electromagnetic radiations.
EOB	Electronic Order of Battle	(U) A list of radar sites and the radar sets or systems that are located at these sites.
EPL	ELINT Parameter Limits	(S) A technical reference document designed, maintained, and promulgated as a national-level guide to support ELINT collection, signal identification and signal analysis activities.
FISINT	Foreign Instrumentation Signals Intelligence	(U) Technical and intelligence information derived from intercept of foreign instrumentation signals which include, but are not limited to, telemetry, beaconry, and electronic interrogators.
GHFS	Global High Frequency System	(U//FOUO) A worldwide network of high-power HF radio stations that provide air/ground HF command and control radio communications between ground agencies and US military aircraft and ships.
HULTEC Database	Hull-to-Emitter Correlation Database	(C) A database of information that fingerprints naval platforms by emitter (ELINT) to platform correlation.
HUNTER		(U) U.S. unmanned aerial vehicle
IA	Information Assurance	n/a
IAD	Information Assurance Directorate	n/a
JPRA	Joint Personnel Recovery Agency	(U) The DoD office of primary responsibility for DoD-wide personnel recovery matters.
JQR	Job Qualifications Requirements	(U) Positional qualification system that establishes the minimum knowledge and skill level required to function effectively at a specific watchstation.
KG-84	n/a	(U) A device that provides for encryption and decryption of data traffic.
KL-43	n/a	(U) A portable off-line text encryption/decryption system ruggedized and intended for use in a tactical environment. Used aboard PACOM SRO aircraft to encrypt short messages for HF transmission.
KLIEGLIGHT	n/a	(U//FOUO) Reporting vehicle used to forward time-sensitive SIGINT technical information to NSOC, SIGINT producers, and Cryptologic Support Groups.
KOI-18	n/a	(U) A small, hand-carried device that reads a standard punched tape and converts the information to a serial output. Used to provide cryptovariables to the KYK-13 or any other compatible equipment

TOP SECRET//COMINT//NOFORN//X1

TOP SECRET//COMINT//NOFORN//X1

Term	Expansion	Definition/Description
KY-58	n/a	(U) A small device that provides secure voice digital communications with FM, AM, VHF, and UHF radios. Designed for mounting in an aircraft instrument panel or radio console.
KYK-13	n/a	(U) A device that stores cryptovariables for transfer to other equipments.
LUNCHBOX	n/a	(U//FOUO) The unclassified nickname for a U.S. Navy PROFORMA processor.
MARTES	n/a	(U//FOUO) Unclassified reference to a collection of software tools for collecting, analyzing and processing signals.
Mission Commander	n/a	(U) An electronic warfare-qualified naval aviator or naval flight officer responsible for all phases of the assigned mission except for matters affecting safety of flight, which remain the exclusive responsibility of the pilot in command.
NATOPS	Naval Air Training and Operating Procedures Standardization	(U) A program governing general flight and operating instructions and procedures applicable to the operation of naval aircraft and related activities.
NICKELBACK	n/a	(U//FOUO) The Joint Chiefs of Staff (JCS) unclassified nickname assigned to COMINT advisory support.
NOIWON	National Operations and Intelligence Watch Officers Network	(U//FOUO) Network of senior watch officers in the Washington area. The NSOC SOO convenes NOIWON conference calls during CRITIC events.
NSG	Naval Security Group	(U) Organization responsible for conducting U.S. Navy Cryptologic operations.
NSGA	Naval Security Group Activity	(U) Third echelon command under Commander, Naval Security Group, e.g., NSGA Misawa. Responsibilities include providing operators in support of air, surface and subsurface collection requirements.
NSOC	National Security Operations Center	(U) 7-day/24-hour watch center for U.S. Cryptologic System activities. Director, NSA/CSS' command-and-control center for time-sensitive operations and focal point for crisis response.
OPNAVINST 3710.7R	Naval Operations Instruction 3710.7R	(U) Chief of Naval Operations instruction that promulgates NATOPS General Flight and Operating Instructions
PA	Public Address	(U) A system of loudspeakers in the EP-3E, driven by the DCMS.
PACROC	Pacific Reconnaissance Operations Center	(U) USCINCPAC coordinating authority for all Sensitive Reconnaissance Operations.
PLA	People's Liberation Army	(U) The entire PRC Military is contained in the People's Liberation Army.
PRC	People's Republic of China	n/a
PREDATOR	n/a	(U) U.S. unmanned aerial vehicle
PROFORMA	n/a	(C) Digital command and control data communications that relay information and instructions to and from radar systems, weapon systems (e.g., surface-to-air missiles, anti-aircraft artillery, fighter aircraft), and control centers.

TOP SECRET//COMINT//NOFORN//X1

Term	Expansion	Definition/Description
PTN	Pacific Tributary Network	(U//FOUO) A dedicated UHF Satellite communications net providing 24-hour voice communications support between national and Pacific theater commands.
RASIN	Radio Signals Notation	(U//FOUO) The COMINT Signal Classification System for classifying and reporting a wide variety of signals with their associated parametrics and characteristics.
RSOC	Regional Security Operations Center	(U) An NSA/CSS operations center that produces SIGINT on a specific region of the world, supporting regional CINCs and warfighters as well as national decision makers.
SCIENCE & TECHNOLOGY (S&T) OPERATOR	n/a	(U) Position designation for Station 20 onboard EP-3E aircraft, normally manned by a Cryptologic Technician Special Signals Operator.
SCARAB	n/a	(U) Commercial name for a ruggedized computer used for the LUNCHBOX PROFORMA processor. Carried onboard the EP-3E.
SENSOR PACER	n/a	(U//FOUO) Nickname assigned to the secure, digital, air-ground-air communications system used for SIGINT reporting and advisory support.
SEVAL	Senior Evaluator	(U) The officer in charge of SIGINT collection operations aboard the EP-3E (Senior Naval Flight Officer)
SOI	Signals Operating Instructions	(U) Target data such as frequencies and call signs that enables communicants to establish and maintain communications.
SOO	Senior Operations Officer	(U) At NSA, the SOO is the senior officer on watch at NSOC. Represents DIRNSA afterhours.
SRO	Sensitive Reconnaissance Operation	(U) Airborne and shipborne platforms operating under the Joint Chiefs of Staff Sensitive Reconnaissance Operation program.
SSA	Special Support Activity	(U) At NSA, the SSA is responsible for disseminating time-sensitive, SIGINT-derived threat warning information and coordinating NICKELBACK support to SRO and other reconnaissance operations.
TACREP	Tactical Report	(U//FOUO) SIGINT-derived reporting vehicle used to provide information on the status of continuing or potential threats, and other events of high interest.
UAV	Unmanned Aerial Vehicle	n/a
USSID	United States Signals Intelligence Directives	(U//FOUO) The mechanism through which the Director, National Security Agency/Chief, Central Security Service exercises operational control of the U.S. SIGINT System
VQ-1	Fleet Air Reconnaissance Squadron One (FAIRECONRON ONE)	(U) U.S. Navy reconnaissance squadron based at NAS Whidbey Island, WA. VQ-1 operated the incident EP-3.
ZEROIZE	n/a	(U) A process that erases the key variable or other stored material, and renders the devices essentially useless and the data unrecoverable.

TOP SECRET//COMINT//NOFORN//X1

TOP SECRET//COMINT//NOFORN//X1

Term	Expansion	Definition/Description
ZIRCON Chat	n/a	(U) A commercial internet relay chat application used on the secure Joint Worldwide Intelligence Communications System network. Allows multiple intelligence providers to communicate with deployed threat warning recipients.

TOP SECRET//COMINT//NOFORN//X1

TOP SECRET//COMINT//NOFORN//X1

Appendix A

(U) Summary of Recommendations

(U) This appendix lists all recommendations in matrix form and suggests a responsible organization for each.

Section Reference	Recommendation / POC
(U) COMINT Equip and Documentation Section 4.2; also 4.3	**Recommendation #1** (U//FOUO) Limit classified and sensitive materials carried onboard SRO platforms to mission-essential materials only. Minimize hardcopy materials in favor of electronic media. POC/Action: NSA and SRO Units
(U) COMINT Equip and Documentation Section 4.2; also 4.3	**Recommendation #2** (U//FOUO) Identify computer hard drives for priority destruction and/or jettison. Mark hard drives with a location for striking to ensure physical destruction. POC/Action: NSA and SRO Units
(U) COMINT Equip and Documentation Section 4.2	**Recommendation #3** (U//FOUO) Eliminate source code from fielded software. POC/Action: NSA and other software originators
(U) COMINT Equip and Documentation Section 4.2	**Recommendation #4** (U//FOUO) Eliminate tape-based recording, replacing it with computer-based recorders with built-in equipment. POC/Action: NSA and SCEs
(U) COMINT Equip and Documentation Section 4.2	**Recommendation #5** (S//SI) Remove processing capability for the HUNTER and PREDATOR UAV and JASSM datalink signals from LUNCHBOX. POC/Action: NSA and Platform Sponsors
(U) COMINT Equip and Documentation Section 4.2	**Recommendation #6** (S) Provide a tailored signals processing capability that fully meets mission requirements for rapid signal detection and identification. POC/Action: NSA
(U) COMINT Equip and Documentation Section 4.2	**Recommendation #7** (U//FOUO) Replace the SCARAB computer key-lock mechanism with a manual quick-release bolt. POC/Action: SRO Units
(U) COMINT Equip and Documentation Section 4.2	**Recommendation #8** (C) Review compromised USSID material to determine if there is a need to change, modify, or update any USSID. POC/Action: NSA
(U) COMINT Equip and Documentation Section 4.2	**Recommendation #9** (S) Continue to monitor PRC communications for evidence of denial and deception activities related to SRO missions. POC/Action: NSA
(U) SIGINT Configuration Mgmt Section 4.4	**Recommendation #10** (U//FOUO) Work with industry and the Intelligence Community to develop and implement safeguard capabilities for SIGINT equipment and materials used by SRO platforms and other SIGINT collection activities at risk. POC/Action: NSA

TOP SECRET//COMINT//NOFORN//X1

TOP SECRET//COMINT//NOFORN//X1

Section Reference	Recommendation / POC
(U) SIGINT Configuration Mgmt Section 4.4	**Recommendation #11** (U//FOUO) Develop and implement configuration controls to govern the use of NSA-deployed software versions and maintain cognizance of field modifications; include procedures to annually overwrite all software with the most currently available software. POC/Action: NSA and SCEs
(U) Cryptographic Materials and Equip Section 5.3	**Recommendation #12** (U//FOUO) Limit COMSEC materials and cryptologic devices onboard deployed platforms to those required to accomplish the platform's mission in a specific timeframe and in a given area of responsibility. POC/Action: SRO Units
(U) Cryptographic Materials and Equip Section 5.3	**Recommendation #13** (U//FOUO) Use electronic key loading devices and leave hardcopy key tape and canisters at the staging base. POC/Action: SRO Units
(U) Cryptographic Materials and Equip Section 5.3	**Recommendation #14** (U//FOUO) Maintain a comprehensive and readily available inventory of all field-deployed COMSEC materials and cryptologic devices. POC/Action: NSA
(U) Cryptographic Materials and Equip Section 5.3	**Recommendation #15** (U) Maintain destruction records and supersession messages at the staging base. POC/Action: SRO Units
(U) Cryptographic Materials and Equip Section 5.3	**Recommendation #16** (S) Continue to refine procedures for timely supersession of GPS worldwide key. POC/Action: SPACECOM
(U) Cryptographic Materials and Equip Section 5.3	**Recommendation #17** (S) Make crosscut shredders available for emergency destruction of keying material. POC/Action: SRO Units and SCEs
(U) Cryptologic Foreign Partner Impact Section 6.3	**Recommendation #18** (U//FOUO) Coordinate notification procedures and notify foreign partners of pertinent information compromised to the PRC. POC/Action: NSA, in coordination with Intelligence Community
(U) Counterintelligence Issues Section 6.5	**Recommendation #19** (U//FOUO) Remove names of all individuals and organizations from forwarding instructions, technical material, and software carried on SRO or other sensitive SIGINT operations. POC/Action: NSA and software providers
(U) Counterintelligence Issues Section 6.5	**Recommendation #20** (U//FOUO) Reduce the amount of personnel information in mission materials to the minimum possible. Do not reference organizations, offices, or names of personnel. POC/Action: SRO Units
(U) U.S. Cryptologic System Crisis Response Section 7.10	**Recommendation #21** (U/FOUO) Implement streamlined NSA policy regarding raw SIGINT. POC/Action: NSA

TOP SECRET//COMINT//NOFORN//X1

Section Reference	Recommendation / POC
(U) U.S. Cryptologic System Crisis Response Section 7.10	**Recommendation #22** (U//FOUO) The Secretary of Defense in coordination with the DCI should charter a damage assessment team within 48 hours of a potential compromise involving DoD assets. The team should serve as the lead for producing findings, damage assessment, and recommendations. POC/Action: OSD/CMS
(U) U.S. Cryptologic System Crisis Response Section 7.10	**Recommendation #23** (C) Implement procedures to increase the SIGINT system's responsiveness during crisis events. POC/Action: NSA
(U) U.S. Cryptologic System Crisis Response Section 7.10	**Recommendation #24** (C) Tie the monitoring of international distress frequencies to specific NICKELBACK advisory conditions. POC/Action: NSA
(U) U.S. Cryptologic System Crisis Response Section 7.10	**Recommendation #25** (U//FOUO) Acquire a record and playback capability immediately for all Pacific Tributary Network (PTN) broadcasts at the KRSOC. POC/Action: NSA
(U) U.S. Cryptologic System Crisis Response Section 7.10	**Recommendation #26** (U//FOUO) Allot sufficient time for intelligence debriefings in order to allow a thorough determination of potentially compromised data. POC/Action: JPRA
(U) U.S. Cryptologic System Crisis Response Section 7.10	**Recommendation #27** (U//FOUO) Incorporate intelligence debriefing into JPRA personnel recovery procedures if there is an Intelligence Community equity. POC/Action: JPRA
(U) U.S. Cryptologic System Crisis Response Section 7.10	**Recommendation #28** (U//FOUO) The Secretary of Defense and the DCI jointly prepare a damage assessment "how to" guide for intelligence compromises. POC/Action: OSD/CMS
(U) Policy Section 8.2	**Recommendation #29** (U//FOUO) Establish written guidance for aircrew actions in the event of hazardous maneuvers by reacting fighters. POC/Action: JCS/CINCs
(U) Policy Section 8.2	**Recommendation #30** (U//FOUO) Provide detailed guidance for Mission Commander and crew actions in the event of a forced landing of the mission aircraft in countries within range of the mission track. POC/Action: JCS/CINCs
(U) Policy Section 8.2 Due: Jan 01	**Recommendation #31** (U//FOUO) Require peacetime detention training for all reconnaissance personnel and personnel engaged in other sensitive operations where there is a risk of detention. POC/Action: SRO Units and SCEs
(U) Policy Section 8.2	**Recommendation #32** (U) Explore pursuing an agreement with the PRC to establish joint procedures to prevent dangerous military activities. POC/Action: JCS/CINCs

TOP SECRET//COMINT//NOFORN//X1

Section Reference	Recommendation / POC
(U) Radio Communications Section 8.3	**Recommendation #33** (U//FOUO) Incorporate guidance into emergency destruction procedures identifying communication equipment that should not be zeroized or destroyed until no longer needed. POC/Action: SRO Units
(U) Radio Communications Section 8.3	**Recommendation #34** (U//FOUO) Train flight crew personnel in the emergency communication procedures used by countries in their areas of operations. POC/Action: Navy Type Commanders, and other service equivalents
(U) Radio Communications Section 8.3	**Recommendation #35** (U//FOUO) Provide guidance in the DoD Flight Information Handbook specific to emergency communications with the PRC and other target nations. POC/Action: NIMA (National Imagery & Mapping Agency) working with Theater CINCs
(U) Internal Communications Section 8.4	**Recommendation #36** (U//FOUO) Improve the performance and intelligibility of the EP-3E PA system to operate better in all environments. POC/Action: NAVAIR
(U) Internal Communications Section 8.4	**Recommendation #37** (U//FOUO) Increase training using helmets during drills so that crew members are proficient at communicating while wearing helmets. POC/Action: SRO Units
(U) Internal Communications Section 8.4	**Recommendation #38** (U//FOUO) Reemphasize the critical role of clear communications between the flight station and aircrew cabin during emergency procedure and Aircrew Coordination Training. POC/Action: SRO Units
(U) Internal Communications Section 8.4	**Recommendation #39** (U//FOUO) Drill emergency crew communications procedures in-flight on a routine basis, practicing reconfiguration of internal communications and alternate communications paths for all combinations of emergencies. POC/Action: SRO Units
(U) Internal Communications Section 8.4	**Recommendation #40** (U//FOUO) As a required part of pre-mission briefings, identify by name key personnel and alternates responsible for leading crew actions and making status reports during emergency destruction. POC/Action: SRO Units
(U) Internal Communications Section 8.4	**Recommendation #41** (U//FOUO) Design and implement improved emergency communications procedures and hardware on the EP-3E to enable reliable communications at all times, especially during abnormal flight conditions. Investigate wireless communications systems. POC/Action: NAVAIR
(U) Classified and Sensitive Material Handling Section 8.5	**Recommendation #42** (S//SI) Ensure the Mission Commander and other personnel responsible for emergency destruction are fully cognizant of the scope and nature of all classified materials onboard the aircraft and are in compliance with USSID 3. POC/Action: SRO Units and SCEs

TOP SECRET//COMINT//NOFORN//X1

TOP SECRET//COMINT//NOFORN//X1

Section Reference	Recommendation / POC
(U) Classified and Sensitive Material Handling Section 8.5	**Recommendation #43** (C) Review USSID 3 requirements for the protection of COMINT systems and data at all classification levels. POC/Action: NSA
(U) Classified and Sensitive Material Handling Section 8.5	**Recommendation #44** (U//FOUO) Issue policy to increase the detail in material inventories to support a rapid and accurate page-for-page reconstruction of all sensitive and classified materials, including all files on hard disks, CD ROMs, and floppy disks. POC/Action: NSA and SCEs
(U) Classified and Sensitive Material Handling Section 8.5	**Recommendation #45** (U//FOUO) Maintain exact backup copies of all electronic media at a ground support facility for every mission. POC/Action: SSO Navy, SRO Units
(U) Classified and Sensitive Material Handling Section 8.5	**Recommendation #46** (U//FOUO) Establish written procedures designating specific ground support personnel who will verify aircraft inventories and electronic media backups prior to every mission. POC/Action: SSO Navy, SRO Units
(U) Classified and Sensitive Material Handling Section 8.5	**Recommendation #47** (C) Review and change, as required, compromised operational information such as radio call signs and frequencies. POC/Action: JCS/CINCs
(U) Emerg Destruction Policy, Procedures, and Training Section 8.6	**Recommendation #48** (U//FOUO) Train aircrew on emergency destruction procedures in a formal setting prior to their operational deployment. POC/Action: SRO units and SCEs
(U) Emerg Destruction Policy, Procedures, and Training Section 8.6	**Recommendation #49** (U//FOUO) Include emergency destruction training, to include both classroom training and in-flight drills, during crew work-ups. Include all crew members from all commands participating in operations. POC/Action: SRO Units
(U) Emerg Destruction Policy, Procedures, and Training Section 8.6	**Recommendation #50** (U//FOUO) Require regular emergency destruction drills during detachments; include situations where destruction procedures are impeded by simultaneous emergencies (e.g., fire of unknown origin, preparations to bail out and/or ditch) and constrained by time limits. POC/Action: SRO Units
(U) Emerg Destruction Policy, Procedures, and Training Section 8.6	**Recommendation #51** (U//FOUO) Include emergency destruction responsibilities and procedures in pre-mission briefings, similar to those for ditching, bailout, and fire of unknown origin. POC/Action: SRO Units
(U) Emerg Destruction Policy, Procedures, and Training Section 8.6	**Recommendation #52** (U//FOUO) Issue individualized written emergency destruction procedures to all crew members prior to flight. POC/Action: SRO Units
(U) Emerg Destruction Policy, Procedures, and Training Section 8.6	**Recommendation #53** (U//FOUO) Include emergency destruction as a sub-area of all positional NATOPS qualifications. POC/Action: Aircraft Model Managers

TOP SECRET//COMINT//NOFORN//X1

TOP SECRET//COMINT//NOFORN//X1

Section Reference	Recommendation / POC
(U) Emerg Destruction Policy, Procedures, and Training Section 8.6	**Recommendation #54** (U//FOUO) Ensure sufficient type and quantity of emergency destruction tools are onboard mission aircraft. POC/Action: NAVAIR, other service equivalents
(U) Emerg Destruction Policy, Procedures, and Training Section 8.6	**Recommendation #55** (U//FOUO) Develop practical procedures for inventorying jettisoned or destroyed materials. POC/Action: NAVAIR, other service equivalents
(U) Emerg Destruction Policy, Procedures, and Training Section 8.6	**Recommendation #56** (U//FOUO) Conduct and document periodic emergency destruction reviews to ensure procedures are current with technology and mission environment changes. POC/Action: SRO Units and SCEs
(U) Emerg Destruction Policy, Procedures, and Training Section 8.6	**Recommendation #57** (U//FOUO) For any equipment not covered by current emergency destruction procedures, require new procedures and training before allowing the equipment onboard. POC/Action: SRO Units, NAVAIR
(U) Emerg Destruction Policy, Procedures, and Training Section 8.6	**Recommendation #58** (U//FOUO) Provide national-level guidance for jettisoning classified materials. POC/Action: JCS
(U) Crew Reaction Section 8.7	**Recommendation #59** (U//FOUO) Review and formalize crew certification procedures for each deploying crew. Include demonstrated ability to execute all emergency procedures satisfactorily, and emergency destruction under less than optimal conditions. POC/Action: SRO Units
(U) Crew Reaction Section 8.7	**Recommendation #60** (U//FOUO) As part of individual qualification, require trainees to exercise and demonstrate proper emergency destruction procedures during in-flight examination. POC/Action: SRO Units
(U) Crew Reaction Section 8.7	**Recommendation #61** (U//FOUO) Examine current organizations with the objective of aligning crew training, cohesion unity, and overall experience. POC/Action: Cryptologic and VQ communities
(U) Systemic Issues Section 9.3	**Recommendation #62** (U//FOUO) Implement, track, and institutionalize the study's recommendations. POC/Action: CNO, DIRNSA, and SCEs

TOP SECRET//COMINT//NOFORN//X1

TOP SECRET//COMINT//NOFORN//X1

Appendix B

(U//FOUO) List of Cryptologic Equipment and Information Compromised

1 <u>**(U) SIGINT Material and Equipment**</u>

1.1 **(U) Policy Documents – USSID Material**

1.1.1 **(U) Hardcopy USSID Material**

(S//SI) The following USSID material was determined to compromised either entirely or partially. Most of the hardcopy USSID material was not carried onboard in its entirety, but was mentioned or partially described in Job Qualification Requirements (JQR), Working Aids, and personal notes. The following material was not destroyed and was left onboard the aircraft in a storage locker.

USSID	Title	Level of Compromise
1	SIGINT Operating policy	Excerpt
3	SIGINT Security Procedures	Excerpts, including Annex A, Section 6 (entire)
9	Host Government Communications	Excerpts and references
18	Legal Compliance & Minimization Procedures	Excerpts and references
101	COMINT Collection Instructions	Excerpts and references
110	Collection Management Procedures	Extensive, including Annex H
205	Standard Technical Report Using Modules (STRUM)	Excerpts and references in Pos 19 tech
212	PROFORMA Signals Processing and Technical Reporting	Excerpts and references in POS 20 tech.
301	Handling of Critical (CRITIC) Information	Extensive, including Annex L
369	Time-Sensitive SIGINT Reporting	Excerpts and references in POS 4 tech material, POS 15 Working Aid, POS 19 Tech
404	Technical Extracts from Traffic Analysis (TEXTA)	Entire USSID, excerpts from TEXTA manual
2846	SIGINT Tasking for USN-846	Extensive excerpts and references in POS 19 Tech

TOP SECRET//COMINT//NOFORN//X1

TOP SECRET//COMINT//NOFORN//X1

| 5511 | Advisory Support to Sensitive Reconnaissance | Detailed description of NICKELBACK conditions and terms, Annex A |

1.1.2 (U) Softcopy USSID Material

(S//SI) Softcopy of the following USSID material was loaded on the COMINT Supervisor's laptop that was left onboard the aircraft. Measures were taken to destroy the laptop (and hard drive). Combining what we know about these efforts, expert testimony, and analysis of the returned laptop, there is a very low likelihood that sensitive cryptologic information could be recovered. As a result, all USSID material listed below is considered as a *possible* compromise.

USSID	Title	Annexes and Changes Included
3	SIGINT Security Procedures	Annex A-F
9	Host Government Communications	
18	Legal Compliance and Minimization Procedures	Annex A-K
107	Burst Signal Recognition & Reporting Procedures	Annex A, B
205	Standard Technical Report Using Modules (SRUM)	Annex A, E
212	PROFORMA Signals Processing and Technical Reporting	Annex A-E
214	Preliminary Mission Summary (PREMS)	
223	PRC Air Communications Activity Reporting	Annex A-C
301	Handling of Critical (CRITIC) Information	Annex A-I
303	SIGINT Reporters' Instructions	SIGINT Reporters' Instructions for: N. Korea AF, Cambodia, Vietnam, Philippines, Thailand
312	SIGINT Reporters' Instructions for the Republics of the Former Soviet Union	
313	Reporting of Distress Signals	
316	Non-Codeword Reporting Program	Annex D North Korean Forces
320	SIGINT Reporters' Instructions for the People's Republic of China	Annex A-F
321	SIGINT Reporters' Instructions for Southeast Asia	
342	PROFORMA Technical Reporting	

TOP SECRET//COMINT//NOFORN//X1

369	Time Sensitive SIGINT Reporting	Annex A, B; changes 1-5
2846	SIGINT Tasking for USN-846	
5511	COMINT Advisory Support to Sensitive Reconnaissance Operations	Annex A-D

1.2 (U) COMINT Material

(S//SI) Hardcopy and softcopy COMINT material was carried onboard the aircraft. The hardcopy material listed below was intact or hand-shredded and left onboard the EP-3E. All material is considered to be compromised.

1.2.1 (S) Hardcopy COMINT Material

	Title	Description
A.	**PRC Air Tech**	Compilation of tech data from multiple sources. Includes the following
A.1	Air Order of Battle (AOB) for PLAAF and PLANAF Air Bases	- Type of aircraft assigned including transports - Number of each Aircraft assigned
A.2	Airfields	Technical data listing document including: - Placename and Placename abbreviation (PNAB) - Geographic coordinates - Identifying data for each airfield - Runway orientation - Atmospheric pressure - Ground controller callsigns - Pilot Billet Suffix (PBS) - Airfield-specific terminology - Subordination
A.3	Maps of Airfields	- Includes current PRC deployments
A.4	Air Frames	- Capabilities - Armament
A.5	PREAMBLE Address Groups (PAGS)	- PLANAF
A.6	Activity Codes	- STRUM - IATS

TOP SECRET//COMINT//NOFORN//X1

.7	<u>Sample Reports</u>	- KLIEGLIGHTs (KL) - Mission Related Technical Summary (MRTS) - STRUM
.8	Civilian Airliners/Transports	- Type - Owner/operator - Home base
A.9	Military navigation call signs and cover numbers	
B.	**PRC Naval Tech**	
B.1	<u>PRC Navy Order of Battle</u>	- PRC Navy Fleet subordination
B.2	Ship weapons/sensors fits	- <u>Capabilities of weapons fits</u>
B.3	Communications and Observations Post/Signal station listing	
.4	Preamble Address Groups (PAGS) listing	- PRC Navy
B.5	Taiwan Navy Tech	- Order of battle - Subordination
.6	Tactical signals and coverterms	
.7	WNP-27 strip (call sign encryption strip)	- Instructions - Historic records (5 year history)
B.8	ELINT associated with PRC Navy vessels	
.9	Map of Spratly Islands	
B.10	<u>Communications Profile</u>	- VHF/HF Frequency List - Channel Numbers - Tactical activity scenarios/identifiers
C.	**Supervisor's Working Aid**	
C.1	Collection Requirement Number (CRN) Tasking	- PRC - N. Korea - Global World
C.2	Intercept Tasking Database (ITDB)	- PRC and Southeastern Asia - Blocks 44-52, 44-53, 44-54
C.3	SRO Mission Track Points	Tracks - 5Q2001 - 5Q2002 - 5Q1000 - 5Q3001

TOP SECRET//COMINT//NOFORN//X1

TOP SECRET//COMINT//NOFORN//X1

C.4	STRUM Codes	-	Air Activity Codes
		-	Naval Activity Codes
C.5	Miscellaneous KL Info	-	FLAGS
		-	CANS
		-	PDDG
C.6	PRC Air Surveillance (ASV)	-	Reacting Airfields
		-	Tracking stations/methods/formats
C.7	VQ-1 Mission Commander's Notebook	-	Advisory notifications summary
C.8	Integrated Air Defense System (IADS)	-	Hand written notes
D	**COMEVAL Brief Binder**		
D.1	Mission Brief	-	Intel Brief
		-	VQ-1 Misawa daily flight schedule
D.2	Airframes/Ships Weapons Fits	-	PRC
		-	Taiwan
D.3	PRC Maps	-	Air bases
		-	SAM Locations
		-	Submarine/Naval combatants
D.4	Taiwan Maps	-	Fighter disposition
		-	Ground attack fighters
D.5	Japanese P-3 Operations Area	-	Maps
E	**Secure Communications Operator (POS 4) Working Aid**		
E.1	POS 4 Start-up procedures		
E.2	Mission Log form	-	Template only
E.3	NICKLEBACK Advisory Codes	-	Summary
E.4	Air Force Advisory Notifications Instruction		
E.5	Message Format Samples	-	Advisory Notification
		-	CRITIC
		-	KLIEGLIGHT
E.6	Standard Operating Procedure for Kadena	-	Callsigns
		-	SIPRNET addresses
F	**Manual Morse Operator (POS 19) Working Aid**		
F.1	SLIPSTICK	-	Azimuth and Range tool

TOP SECRET//COMINT//NOFORN//X1

TOP SECRET//COMINT//NOFORN//X1

F.2	PRC/Vietnam Tech	- Air Order of Battle - Tracking Methods
F.3	PRC Defensive Position Reports	- 5Q1000 - 5Q2001 - 5Q2002
F.4	Maps	- South China Sea - Taiwan Strait
F.5	PRC ASV & Air Order of Battle	- AZ/Range, All-China Grid, Special Reporting Grid - Arbitrary Unit Designators - WAJAD-9 - N-12 Cipher System - Basic Callsign System
F.6	Vietnamese ASV & Air Order of Battle	- Arbitrary Unit Designators
F.7	Manual Morse Breakouts	
G	**S&T Special Signals Operator (POS 20) Tech**	
G.1	General PROFORMA Info/Descriptions	- MARKHAM - FOREJUDGE - SAM HEARTBURN - NOVELETTE - RSBN
G.2	Pacific Theater Top Twenty Signals Search Priorities	- PRC signals only
G.3	Air Order of Battle	- PRC and Vietnam
G.4	TEXSIG descriptions	- XXS S9337 - XXS K4311 - XXS K4318 - XXS K4331
H	**Airborne Cryptologic Direct Support Element (CSDE) Senior Operator Study Module**	
H.1	Mission Tracks	- 5Q2001 - 5Q2002 - 5Q1000
H.2	Taiwan TACAIR Working Aid	- Air Order of Battle - Aircraft/Armament/ELINT - Airfields/Coordinates/Runway orientation - Ground Controller Recoveries - Aircraft callsigns/prefixes, including NATO

TOP SECRET//COMINT//NOFORN//X1

TOP SECRET//COMINT//NOFORN//X1

		- Top 20 Frequency lists - Known and recovered frequencies - Taiwan Air Defense Identification Zone
H.3	Taiwan Navy Order of Battle	- Basic Naval tactics - Pictures of naval entities
I	**Forms Folder**	
I.1	KLIEGLIGHT Format	- Template only
I.2	STRUM Format	- Template only
I.3	PREM format	- Template only
I.4	Cond3/ Cond3 Summary NICKLEBACK	- Template only
I.5	Cond 4 NICKLEBACK	- Template only
I.6	Morse Auto KL	- Template only
J	**Airborne Direct Support Operations Chinese Navy Operator– JQR Signature Sheet (10 Oct 98)**	- Signature list of training topics - Contains references to classified online working aids at NAIC, CTEP, and KRSOC - Some hand-written notes included
K	**Airborne Direct Support Operations Chinese Navy Operator - Study Guide (10 Oct 98)**	- PLAN Mission, threat, disputes - PLAN Organization - Shore installations - Flotillas and squadrons - Combatant Order-of-Battle - Auxiliaries, numbering system, prefixes - VHF communications procedures - Tactical Maneuvering Communications Procedures - Tactical Activities (submarine, anti-surface/anti-air, - HF communications (HF voice/manual Morse, RIBBED (COZY III), National/fleet support broadcast - Geography - Missile systems
L	**Airborne Fleet Operations Chinese Intermediate JQR**	- Signature list of training topics - Contains references to classified online working aids at NSA
L.1	Target Training Package: Submarine Launched Ballistic Missile Activity	- Organization, launch platforms, missile system, Areas of Operation, past SLBM launches - Missile testing operations - Communications - Vocabulary

TOP SECRET//COMINT//NOFORN//X1

L.2	Target Training Package: Air-to-Surface Attack	- PRC Aircraft (fighters and helicopters) description and armament - Range communications - Attack Phase - Vocabulary
L.3	Map of PRC airfields	
M	**Airborne Direct Support Operations CHILING TAC AIR Operator – JQR Signature Sheet & Study Guide (15 Sept 97)**	- USN-846 overview (including supported Aircraft, SRO missions, Track numbers, fleet support missions) - EP-3E organization (positions, relationships) - Tasking and associated activities - Reporting (internal, external, CRITIC) - COMINT Advisory Support and conditions - USSID descriptions (3, 18, 101, 150, 313, 320) - PRC Air Defense (Mission, Air surveillance) - PRC Air Order of Battle (TEXTA Manual, Units & locations, Geography) - PRC Aircraft including indicators - Activity (local airfield, basic flight, combat training, reactions, live intercept, defensive patrols, navigation training and inter-airfield flights, bomber activity) - Transcription requirements
N	**Manual Morse Refresher (POS 19)**	- JQR Signature sheet
N.1	Advisory Support Operations Information (NICKELBACK)	- Includes ground sites who can issue external conditions
N.2	Mission Covernames and descriptions	- BEGGAR HAWK - BEGGAR SHADOW - CAPSULE JACK - DISTANT WIND - DISTANT SENT
O	**COMEVAL JQR SIGNATURE SHEET**	- Signature list of training topics with detailed notes on items (listed below)
O.1	Airborne Reconnaissance Fundamentals	- USCINCPAC Manual 5157 notes - Advisory Support (NICKELBACK) terminology - Ground Unit ADSO support - SRO platforms and mission descriptions - Mission numbers and operating areas - Squadron locations and collection capabilities

TOP SECRET//COMINT//NOFORN//X1

TOP SECRET//COMINT//NOFORN//X1

O.2	North Korea Tech Material	- NKAF Air Order of Battle - NKAF Fighter/Bomber characteristics - SAM indications and sites - Map of NKAF significant placenames
O.3	Hand-written notes in JQR	- USSID identification - Radio/telephone procedures - U.S. Fleet organization - Command/MCOC organization - Warfighter Communications paths (TRE, TRAP, TDDS, TOPS, TIBS) - COMINT releasability caveats (SEABOOT, SETTEE, KAMPUS, DRUID, RORIPA, NOFORN, ORCON) - Callsign definitions - NK Air Defense System - NK SAM force - UNACCENTED description (not in detail) - NK MRBM Launch indicators - NK Reacting Airfields - NK Infiltration Operations - PRC Airfields and aircraft locations - PRC Reacting Airfields - PRC Naval Auxiliary vessel classes - PRC ASV Tracking Stations - Russian PACOFAF, PVO/TAF, and SAF Airfields - Russian Naval Base missions and orders of battle - Russian weapons range activities - Russian aircraft, weapons and associated ELINT /PROFORMA - Russian Surface Order of Battle - Russian missiles, platforms, ELINT, ranges - Russian SA-10B Group of Battalions reactions and associated ELINT - Russian Case notation break-out - ONAZN-004 System, CER break-out - Russian reaction/exercise scenarios - Taiwan aircraft/combatants including mission, weapons, associated ELINT - Vietnam airfields/naval bases including mission and order of battle - Vietnam aircraft including mission, weapons, and associated ELINT - Vietnam threat airfields - Spratley Islands re-supply operations

TOP SECRET//COMINT//NOFORN//X1

TOP SECRET//COMINT//NOFORN//X1

O.4	Special Signals Guide	- Signals terminology - POS 20 equipment descriptions - Publications descriptions (RASIN manual, COTS manual, COMINT Parameters List, Search Environment List, PROFORMA Signals index) - References to enciphered and scrambled speech, cellular, short duration signal, ALE, low probability of intercept - PROFORMA signal descriptions, coverterms and associated target countries.

1.2.2 (U) Softcopy COMINT Material

(S//SI) The COMINT Supervisor's laptop contained softcopy COMINT material (as well as USSID material detailed previously). The material listed below is considered as a *possible* compromise, given our assessment that there is a very low likelihood of recovering data from the laptop.

A	COMINT Supervisor's Laptop	Description
A.1	Various Classified Webpages	<u>Classified Webpages from internal NSA web</u> - Includes numerous names of individuals - Internal web address information - Extensive information about KRSOC
A.2	North Korean Tech Material	- N. Korean grid key/SPC page recoveries (Apr 99) - DSA Technical Information Report (32-1-99) - N. Korean East and West Coast Voice (Case, Callsign, Class, AUD) - N. Korean East and West Coast Morse (Case, Callsign, ID, AUD) - N. Korean ELINT notations
A.3	Floppy Disk	- STRUMS (previous 24 months) - Partial PREMS (previous 6 months)

1.3 (U) COMINT Systems

(S) The COMINT equipment onboard the aircraft was generally unclassified with the exception of two carry-on computers, a SCARAB computer containing the LUNCHBOX PROFORMA processor and a laptop containing MARTES analysis tools. All data resident on these two systems is considered compromised.

TOP SECRET//COMINT//NOFORN//X1

TOP SECRET//COMINT//NOFORN//X1

	Item	Description
A	SCARAB Computer	- LUNCHBOX PROFORMA Processor - XBIT Signals Analysis software (bit manipulation) - BLACKMAGIC Demodulation software
B	MARTES Laptop	- MARTES (COMINT version 1999.0.2) - RASIN Manual - RASIN Manual Working Aid - Telegraphic Codes Manual

1.4 (U) ELINT Material

(S) Hardcopy and softcopy ELINT material was carried onboard the aircraft. The list of materials below was left onboard the EP-3E, either intact or hand-shredded, and is considered compromised.

1.4.1 (S) Hardcopy ELINT Material

	Item	Description
A	**NRO Radar Fingerprinting document**	- Australian MoD draft report on AN/ULQ-16 employment - AN/ULQ-16 wiring diagrams - Radar fingerprinting techniques and procedures - Precise radar parametric data for USCGC Jarvis
B	**Lab Operator Standard Notebook**	
B.1	Standard ELINT operating procedures	- Signal logging and reporting procedures - TACELINT message format - Standard location and signal annotation abbreviations
B.2	ELINT recording procedures	- Procedures for recording, annotating, and forwarding recorded wideband signals
B.3	EOB downloading procedures	- Downloading and formatting procedures for MIDB EOB data at http://luna.diac.dia.ic.gov/DBAinfonet/DOWNLOAD/Files/help.html
B.4	Sonobuoy exploitation notes	- Russian sonobuoy interrogation data formats and audio frequencies
B.5	Surface-to-Air Missile (SAM) and Surface-to-Surface Missile (SSM) notes	- Association of ELNOTs with missile fire control radars, beacons, seekers, and illuminators - Missile guidance signal format notes

TOP SECRET//COMINT//NOFORN//X1

TOP SECRET//COMINT//NOFORN//X1

		- Association of PROFORMA signals with missile systems
C	**Lab Operator Trainee Study Notes (POS 10)**	
C.1	Russian Far East Military District (FEMD) Air Order of Battle	- Association of fighter and bomber aircraft with airfields - Standard aircraft weapon and radar fits - Association of ELNOTs with NATO names and standard parametric bands of radars
C.2	Russian FEMD Naval Order of Battle	- Standard combatant surface vessel weapon fits - Standard submarine ballistic and cruise missile fits - Association of ELNOTs with NATO names and standard parametric bands of radars
C.3	Russian SAM notes	- U.S. doctrinal ranges of Russian SAM systems - Association of ELNOTs with NATO names and standard parametric bands of SAM associated radars.
C.4	PRC Air Order of Battle	- Association of fighter and bomber aircraft with major airfields in the Shenyang, Beijing, Jinan, Nanjing, and Guangzhou Military Regions - Standard aircraft weapon and radar fits - Association of ELNOTs with NATO and commercial names and standard parametric bands of radars
C.5	PRC Naval Order of Battle	- Surface vessel weapon fits for combatant vessels of frigate size and larger, by hull - Association of submarines, by hull, to operational bases - Association of ELNOTs with NATO and commercial names and PRC military designations of maritime radars - Standard parametric bands of PRC maritime radars
D	**SEVAL and Mission Commander Brief Binders**	- Identical to COMEVAL Brief Binder
D.1	Mission Brief	- Intel Brief - VQ-1 Misawa daily flight schedule
D.2	Airframes/Ships Weapons Fits	- PRC - Taiwan

TOP SECRET//COMINT//NOFORN//X1

D.3	PRC Maps	- Air bases - SAM Locations - Submarine/Naval combatants
D.4	Taiwan Maps	- Fighter disposition - Ground attack fighters
D.5	Japanese P-3 Operations Area	- Maps
E	**Mission Chart**	- SRO Track 5Q2002 coordinates
F	**ELINT Parameter Limits (EPL)**	- September 2000 Yellow EPL - March 1999 Blue EPL - Both manually updated through Feb 2001

1.4.2 (U) Softcopy ELINT Material

(S) The ELINT Evaluator's laptop computer was destroyed by the crew and left onboard the aircraft. The laptop hard drive was recovered, though not found with the laptop. Both were analyzed by NSA experts and it was determined that the hard drive probably survived crew destruction attempts only to be copied and then destroyed by the PRC. All data resident on this system is considered compromised. A zip disk and floppy disk from the Lab Operator's position were also compromised.

	Item	Description
A	**ELINT Evaluator's Laptop Computer**	
A.1	Electronic Order of Battle (EOB)	- Derived from EOB-LITE in late 2000. Contained worldwide radar location data.
A.2	VQ-1 Mission Commander Notebook	- Squadron specific guidance for implementation of USSID 5511 and CINCPACINST 5157 SRO requirements - SRO Track coordinates for all VQ-1 tracks - Misc. message templates - COMINT Sanitization Primer - AN/ALQ-108 OPSEC and employment guidance - PREMS (previous 6 months)
B	**Lab Operator Zip Disk**	
B.1	Collector Technical ELINT Guidance Manual (CTEGM)	- Version dated 28 February 2000
B.2	HULTEC Database	- Pacific HULTEC database derived from JICPAC database
B.3	Electronic Order of Battle (EOB)	- Derived from DIA EOB-LITE in February 2001. Contained worldwide radar location data.

C		**Lab Operator Floppy Disk**		
	C.1	TACELINT Reports	-	Misc. VQ-1 TACELINT reports for February - March 2001 from PACOM AOR
			-	Misc. VQ-1 TACELINT reports for October - December 2000 from CENTCOM AOR

1.4.3 (U) ELINT Systems

(S) The bulk of the ELINT systems are off-the-shelf devices that, although designed for the ELINT mission, contain no particularly sensitive technologies. Two systems that represent a specific concern include the AN/ULQ-16 and the AN/ALQ-108.

	Item	**Description**
A	AN/ALQ-108	- Passive and active exploitation of early Soviet IFF and range extension signals
B	AN/ULQ-16	- Precise radar pulse timing measurements

2. (U) COMSEC Material and Equipment

2.1 (U) COMSEC Material

(S) Keying material and other cryptographic material were taken onboard the EP-3E. The following items were hand-torn, remained onboard the aircraft, and are considered compromised. All keying material (with the exception of GPS world wide key) was superseded within 15 hours. The GPS was superseded within 11 days.

	Item	**Dates/Segment**
A.	AKAA 283 MARK XII Mode 3/A	31 Mar, 01 Apr
B.	AKAC 1553 TRIAD Numeral Cipher	31 Mar, 01 Apr
C.	AKAC L506USAF TRIAD Cipher	31 Mar, 01 Apr
D.	AKAL L506 USAF Strategic Operations TRIAD Airborne MATRIX Authentication System	31 Mar, 01 Apr
E.	USKAC 374 USPACOM OPSCODE	April
F.	AKAK A4001 PACAF KL-43 Key	31 Mar, 01 Apr
G.	AKAT 3662 KI-1B/1C Punched tape	31 Mar, A&B
H.	AKAT A5523 KG-40A OP KEY	31 Mar, 01 Apr
I.	AKAT G2747 KY-57/58 OP KEY	Segments 3 & 4
J.	AKAT G2748 KY-57/58 OP KEY	Segments 3 & 4
K.	USKAT 1105 KY-57/58 OP KEY	31 Mar, 01 Apr
L.	USKAT 1619 KY-57/58 OP KEY	31 Mar, 01 Apr

TOP SECRET//COMINT//NOFORN//X1

M.	USKAT 20415 ANDVT OPKEY	31 Mar, 01 Apr
N.	USKAT A5503 KG-40A OP KEY	31 Mar
O.	USKAT B5697 KYV-5 OP KEY	31 Mar, 01 Apr
P.	USKAT 12228 KG-84 OP KEY	31 Mar, 01 Apr

2.2 (U) COMSEC Equipment

(S) The following equipment was left onboard the aircraft. The recovery team determined that the equipment was at a minimum examined by the PRC. There were signs of PRC intrusion into many pieces of equipment that could indicate PRC attempts at reverse engineering.

	Title	**Description**
A.	KY58 - 8 units	Secure Voice encryption device
B.	KG-84 - 2 units	Secure Data encryption device
C.	KL-43 - 1 unit	Off-line encryption device
D.	KIR-1C - 1 unit	Identify Friend or Foe (IFF)
E.	KIT-1C - 1 unit	Identify Friend or Foe (IFF)
F.	KG-40 - 1 unit	Secure Data encryption device
G.	KGX-40 - 1 unit	Remote control unit for KG-40
H.	KOI-18 - 2 units	Common fill device
I.	KYV-5 - 2 units	VACTOR Secure Voice encryption device (ANDVT)

TOP SECRET//COMINT//NOFORN//X1

TOP SECRET//COMINT//NOFORN//X1

Appendix C

(U//FOUO) Cryptologic Foreign Partner Impact

(C) The EP-3 Assessment Team requested that NSA's Office of Foreign Relations provide information on the impact of the EP-3E compromise to NSA's cryptologic foreign partners. This appendix provides NSA's response and identifies internal actions that NSA will take to notify foreign partners.

(U) NSA Office of Foreign Relations Determinations

(TS//SI) After reviewing materials provided by the EP-3 Assessment Team, the Office of Foreign Relations has determined that the impact to NSA's foreign relations program is low. We have identified below areas of potential compromise, recommended actions, and due dates for those actions. No prior coordination with other Intelligence Community or other US government officials, unless otherwise noted in the recommended action, is required. The Office of Foreign Relations will advise the DCI/Special Assistant for Foreign Intelligence Relationships of this information. The Office of Foreign Relations and the Director, NSA will coordinate the release of this information to other national civilian, military and Intelligence Community authorities in any summary reports, briefings, or presentations.

(U//FOUO) Areas of Potential Compromise and Recommended Actions

1. (TS//SI) Fact of the following SIGINT relationships and associated releasability caveats:
    * South Korea (KAMPUS, SETTEE, SEABOOT)
    * Japan (RORIPA)
    * Taiwan
    * Canada
    * Australia
    * New Zealand
    * United Kingdom

Action: (TS//SI) The Office of Foreign Relations will request via formal message that incountry NSA SIGINT representatives meet with partner agency counterparts to advise them of the compromise, in the cases of South Korea, Taiwan, and Japan, since those relationships are classified and protected in those nations. The Commonwealth relationships are unclassified. DUE: NLT 31 July 2001

2. (S//SI) Existence of airborne reconnaissance sharing programs with:
    * United Kingdom (NIMROD)
    * Japan (Project ARIEL)

TOP SECRET//COMINT//NOFORN//X1

TOP SECRET//COMINT//NOFORN//X1

Action: (S//SI) The Office of Foreign Relations will request via formal message that incountry NSA SIGINT representatives coordinate with in-country USN representatives an approach to the host-nation SIGINT and naval partners. In the case of Japan, in-country coordination with COS Tokyo is also recommended. The Office of Foreign Relations will request a summary from in-country representatives of their activities in this regard. DUE: NLT 31 August 2001

3. (C) NSA procedures for targeting of host nation communications (USSID 9).

Action: (C) The Office of Foreign Relations recommends no action be initiated with foreign governments. If leaked, the Office of Foreign Relations recommends in general that a position of not commenting on the details of US intelligence activities be maintained, but reserves the right to respond on a case-by-case basis to certain partner nations. DUE: N/A

4. (TS//SI) Specific EP-3 targeting of Taiwan:

Action: (TS//SI) The Office of Foreign Relations will request via formal message that the in- country NSA SIGINT representative in Taiwan advise the partner and other pertinent Taiwanese intelligence and intelligence policy leadership that signals information regarding Taiwanese military forces were compromised. The in-country representative will emphasize to the partner that this type of information was on-board for situational awareness reasons. The Office of Foreign Relations will request via email that the SIGINT Directorate coordinate with the Naval Security Group for the compilation of a list of the specific information compromised. The SIGINT Directorate will provide via appropriate means this information to the in-country NSA representative for passage to the Taiwanese partner. Concurrently, the Director of Foreign Relations will advise the senior Taiwanese representative in the United States of the compromise. DUE: NLT 31 July 2001

5. (S//SI) Targeting of PROFORMA signals of a multitude of nations

Action: (S//SI) The Office of Foreign Relations recommends no action be initiated with foreign governments. If leaked, the Office of Foreign Relations recommends in general that a position of not commenting on the details of US intelligence activities be maintained, but reserves the right to respond on a case-by-case basis to certain partner or Allied nations. The Office of Foreign Relations on a case-by-case basis may advise them that this type of information was on- board to provide situational / threat awareness information to the aircraft. We may note that US and other Allied PROFORMA data was included in the equipment. DUE: N/A

6. (S//SI) Fact of staging of US Navy EP-3 missions from Thailand and associated targets (India/ Pakistan)

Action: (TS//SI) The Office of Foreign Relations will request via formal message that the NSA representative in Thailand advise the US Embassy country team of this

TOP SECRET//COMINT//NOFORN//X1

TOP SECRET//COMINT//NOFORN//X1

compromise. We do not believe the Thai partner SIGINT agency or government should be advised of the compromise, because of the newness of the current partner leadership and the tenuous political situation in Thailand. The Office of Foreign Relations recommends no action be initiated with Indian or Pakistani partner governments regarding the existence or origination of these flights or of the targeting of their communications. In-country NSA representatives in India and Pakistan will be apprised via email of the compromise and asked to advise respective COS's and US Embassy country teams for their background. If leaked, the Office of Foreign Relations recommends that a position of not commenting on the details of US intelligence activities be maintained. DUE: NLT 31 July 2001

7. (S//SI) PRC target data routinely shared with Asian and other partners

Action: (S//SI) The Office of Foreign Relations will request via email that the SIGINT Directorate, using appropriate means, advise foreign partners involved in the targeting of PRC communications of the compromise of PRC target data, in order to prepare these partners for potential SOI changes. DUE: NLT 31 July 2001

8. (S//SI) EP-3-based collection technology possibly also on partner EP-3 platforms

Action: (S//SI) The Office of Foreign Relations will request that the EP-3 Assessment Team with the Naval Security Group identify compromised equipment similar to that on-board partner EP-3 aircraft and develop appropriate presentations for foreign SIGINT and naval partners. At that time an assessment regarding foreign partner approaches can be made together with the EP-3 Assessment Team and the Naval Security Group. DUE: NLT 31 July 2001

9. (U//FOUO) Australian SIGINT partner tasking message

Action: (U//FOUO) The Office of Foreign Relations has already advised DSD via email to in-country US liaison personnel, as to the particular compromise. No further action required. DUE: N/A

10. (C) Fact of US SIGINT System and/or EP-3 targeting of India, Pakistan, Malaysia, Philippines, and Sri Lanka

Action: (S//SI) The Office of Foreign Relations recommends no action be initiated with these foreign governments, only two of which are SIGINT partners. We will request via email that in-country NSA representatives in India and Pakistan advise their respective COS's and Embassy country teams, but not the partner governments, of the potential compromise. No further action is required. If leaked, the Office of Foreign Relations recommends that a position of not commenting on the details of US intelligence activities be maintained. DUE: NLT 31 July 2001

TOP SECRET//COMINT//NOFORN//X1

TOP SECRET//COMINT//NOFORN//X1

11. (C) Fact of geographic areas of DSD, GCHQ, and CSE TEXTA authority; Compromise of GCHQ RASIN Manual Working Aid; CSE Telegraphic Codes Manual; DSD document on AN/ULQ-16 Operations at Kangaroo 95 (ADF exercise).

Action: (S//SI) The Office of Foreign Relations will request via email that NSA in-country representatives advise these Second Party partners of these compromises. No further action is required. DUE: 31 July 2001

TOP SECRET//COMINT//NOFORN//X1

TOP SECRET//COMINT//NOFORN//X1

Appendix D

(U) Destruction Testing Procedures

(C) This appendix provides the destruction testing procedures used in an attempt to recreate the crew's destruction of three pieces of equipment: the SCARAB computer, which was loaded with the LUNCHBOX PROFORMA system, the MARTES laptop, and the COMINT Supervisor's laptop. Conclusions drawn from the testing are also discussed.

I. (U//FOUO) **General Practices**
   a. An Aberdeen Test Center staff member served as the Test Director.
   b. The Test Director will instrument and measure the shock inflicted on the devices under test (DUT) as well as possible given the size of the different devices and the severity of the destruction. A video record will be captured of the tests.
   c. The physical structures involved in the destruction (the floor, chairs, tabletops) have been recreated. Some care has been taken to assure that the DUTs will not fly off the test platforms and benefit from any unintended shock.
   d. At each juncture of the test, the computer hard disks will be replaced with fresh disks to determine at what point most damage was inflicted. The disks will be returned for analysis immediately following the test. At that time, a preliminary examination will determine if the disks will be viable for recovery.

II. (C) **SCARAB Computer**
   e. For the SCARAB re-creation, we have procured a single SCARAB computer. We have a series of four tests to perform on the SCARAB, and will have to perform them on the same housing, although we will be trading out disks at various stages of the test.
   f. The SCARAB will never be powered up during the test sequence.
   g. There will be a series of accelerated drop tests performed in the following manner:
      i. The DUT will be manually lifted to approximately 5ft and sent to the floor with positive force. The exact amount of force will be hard to duplicate but will be measured by the instrumentation.
      ii. After the first drop, the computer disk will be removed and replaced.
      iii. Then a series of four accelerated drops will be performed, after which the computer disk will be removed.
      iv. Then repeat the single and quad drops, totaling four tests (four disks for analysis).
      v. If at anytime the SCARAB is damaged to the point that similar mechanical stresses cannot be re-created, the testing will cease.
   h. In each of the accelerated drop tests, the SCARAB will always land on its bottom or back edge. In particular, the first drop will land on the bottom edge where the removable drive is mounted.

TOP SECRET//COMINT//NOFORN//X1

TOP SECRET//COMINT//NOFORN//X1

    i. The test will not attempt to recreate the kicking that occurred between drops.
    j. The following hard drives will be used in the following sequences:
        i. Test – 1: Seagate MEDALIST ST34520W; S#AYQ30730
        ii. Test – 2: Seagate MEDALIST ST34520W; S#AYS24316
        iii. Test – 3: Seagate MEDALIST ST34520W; S#AYS55957

III. (C) **MARTES Laptop** – Tadpole Ultrabook IIi
    k. For the POS20 laptop re-creation, we have traded new Tadpole Ultrabook laptops for used inventory, which were of the same generation as the computer in question. Record the laptop serial number and identity of each of the hard disks, noting which disks are used for each of the two tests. There are two disks in the Tadpole. Refer to disk1 as the disk closest to the front left side, and disk2 as the disk in the middle left of the computer. Note disk1 will be the bootable disk and disk2 will be a "data" disk.
        i. Laptop S# U40-1347
        ii. Test-1; Hard disk1 S# GZLE1332
        iii. Test-1; Hard disk2 S# GZLE8015
        iv. Test-2; Hard disk1 S# GZLD6396
        v. Test-2; Hard disk2 S# GZLE4022
    l. There are two basic tests that will be performed on one of the laptops. The second laptop will be held in spare as well as used to verify the operation of the disks after they have been tested and analyzed for the purposes of recovery.
    m. The laptop will have been powered-on, and the lid closed with a user logged into the computer, for five minutes prior to the recreation. The intent is to allow the computer to reach any suspended state, which would have occurred after the laptop lid had closed and other activities had taken place.
    n. Test sequence:
        i. Tabletop drop to the floor after bouncing off the seat of a chair.
        ii. Replace the hard disks.
        iii. Leaning the closed laptop against a simulated chair rail, where the laptop is the hypotenuse of a triangle formed with the floor and the chair rail. Bottom of the laptop touching the rail.
        iv. Stomp with one foot on the keyboard until the laptop is broken into pieces. Should be performed by person weighing 180 to 200 pounds.
        v. Remove the hard disks for analysis.

IV. (C) **COMINT Supervisor's Laptop** – Gateway Solo 2500
    o. For the POIC laptop re-creation, we have procured two refurbished Gateway Solo 2550 laptops. They differ in a few areas such as processor speed and amount of RAM. The battery, floppy, and hard disk are mounted in the same locations on the test systems as with the fielded system, but are secured in slightly difference fashion. Specifically, it is described that with the removal of the single screw visible on the bottom surface of the laptop, the hard disk can slide from the side of the Solo 2500. This same action on the Solo 2550 only removes a plastic cover and requires the removal of two more screws before the drive will slide out. This is not expected to have much of an impact on the

TOP SECRET//COMINT//NOFORN//X1

re-creation, but it is likely to prevent the hard disk from coming loose during the stomping tests.
p. Record the laptop serial number and identity of each of the hard disks, noting which disks are used for each of the two tests.
  i. Laptop S# B2500380397
  ii. Test-1; Hard disk S# T607E59247
  iii. Test-2; Hard disk S# 5J08870645
q. There are two basic tests that will be performed on one of the laptops. The second laptop will be held in spare as well as used to verify the operation of the disks after they have been tested and analyzed for the purposes of recovery.
r. The laptop will have been powered-on, and the lid open with a user logged into the computer, for five minutes prior to the recreation. The intent is to allow the computer to reach any suspended state, which would have occurred after the laptop flipped into one of the F-racks and other activities had taken place.
s. Test sequence:
  i. Hold the laptop with the keyboard side facing down. The screen will then be hit on the surface of a table top (face down) with the desired effect to crack the spine leaving the screen bent approximately 25 degrees past the horizontal position.
  ii. Replace the hard disk.
  iii. Drop the laptop to the chair rails, face up, such that the back of the display is on one chair rail and the bottom of the laptop is on the other.
  iv. Stomp with one foot on the keyboard until the laptop is broken into pieces. Should be performed by person weighing 180 to 200 pounds.
  v. Remove the hard disk for analysis.

V. (C) Results and Conclusions

(C) Generally, results from the re-created destruction tests revealed the difficulty of disabling a computer system with shock by dropping, stomping, or striking the equipment. For each of the three systems tested, results did not damage the computers enough to conclude that data recovery was impossible. This underscores the importance of providing clear instructions and training for how to physically destroy computers.

(C) In the end, the EP-3 Team relied on the examination of the recovered computers from the returned EP-3E aircraft as the primary basis for estimating the recoverability of data. Results from the destruction tests were used as supporting data.

TOP SECRET//COMINT//NOFORN//X1

Appendix E

(U) EP-3E Radio Equipment and Networks

(U) Radio Equipment

(U) The EP-3E is equipped with a variety of radio transmitter/receivers (transceivers).

(U//FOUO) Two AN/ARC-94 HF radios are provided for long-range communication. One (HF-1) is configured for secure modem communications and is encrypted using a KG-84C encryption device. The other (HF-2) is configured for voice communications and can be encrypted using a KYV-5 encryption device.

(U//FOUO) Three AN/ARC-206 radios are provided for UHF line-of-sight communications. UHF-1 and UHF-2 are controlled by the SEVAL and are configured for voice communications. Both can be encrypted using KY-58 encryption devices. A third AN/ARC-206 radio is configured for line-of-sight datalink operations.

(U//FOUO) Two AN/ARC-182 radios are provided for VHF or UHF line-of-sight communications. Both are controlled from the flight station and are configured for voice communications. Both can be encrypted using KY-58 encryption devices. The control units for these radios have a switch setting allowing an easy and immediate change to the emergency frequency (243.0 MHz or 121.5 MHz) associated with the frequency band in use. A separate switch setting overrides the selected frequency band and tunes directly to 243.0 MHz.

(U//FOUO) One LST-5 satellite radio is provided for secure UHF voice satellite communications. The radio can only be controlled locally at its location in an avionics bay inside the aircraft cabin. It is encrypted using a KY-58 encryption device.

(U//FOUO) The OL-390 Digital Communications Group and its associated UHF radio are used for secure satellite modem communications. The radio is controlled by the secure communications operator and is encrypted using a KG-84A encryption device. This radio shares distribution and antenna equipment with the LST-5; simultaneous transmission using both radios is not possible.

(U) Radio Networks

(S) The Global High Frequency System (GHFS) is a worldwide network of high-power HF stations that provides air/ground HF command and control radio communications between ground agencies and U.S. military aircraft. The GHFS network supports SRO aircraft by passing encoded NICKELBACK advisory conditions, position reports and administrative traffic.

TOP SECRET//COMINT//NOFORN//X1

TOP SECRET//COMINT//NOFORN//X1

(S) The Pacific Tributary Network (PTN) is a UHF secure voice satellite network that provides COMINT advisory support and threat warning to U.S. and allied forces in the theater. Net participants include the Pacific Reconnaissance Operations Center (PACROC), which provides coordination and flight following to SRO aircraft, KRSOC, and NSOC/SSA.

(S) The SENSOR PACER network is a UHF secure low data-rate digital satellite network that provides time-sensitive SIGINT reporting, COMINT advisory support, threat warning, and administrative traffic support to SRO assets worldwide. Net participants include KRSOC and the Tactical SIGINT Interaction Center at Kadena AB, Okinawa (TSIC-K).

(S) The SIERRA ONE Early Warning network is a UHF secure voice satellite network utilized by 5th and 7th Fleet P-3's and EP-3E's for tactical reporting and coordination. Net participants include all PACOM Tactical Support Centers (TSC) and CTF 57/72, Kami Seya, Japan.

TOP SECRET//COMINT//NOFORN//X1

TOP SECRET//COMINT//NOFORN//X1

Appendix F   (U) Schematic of EP-3E with Position Identifications

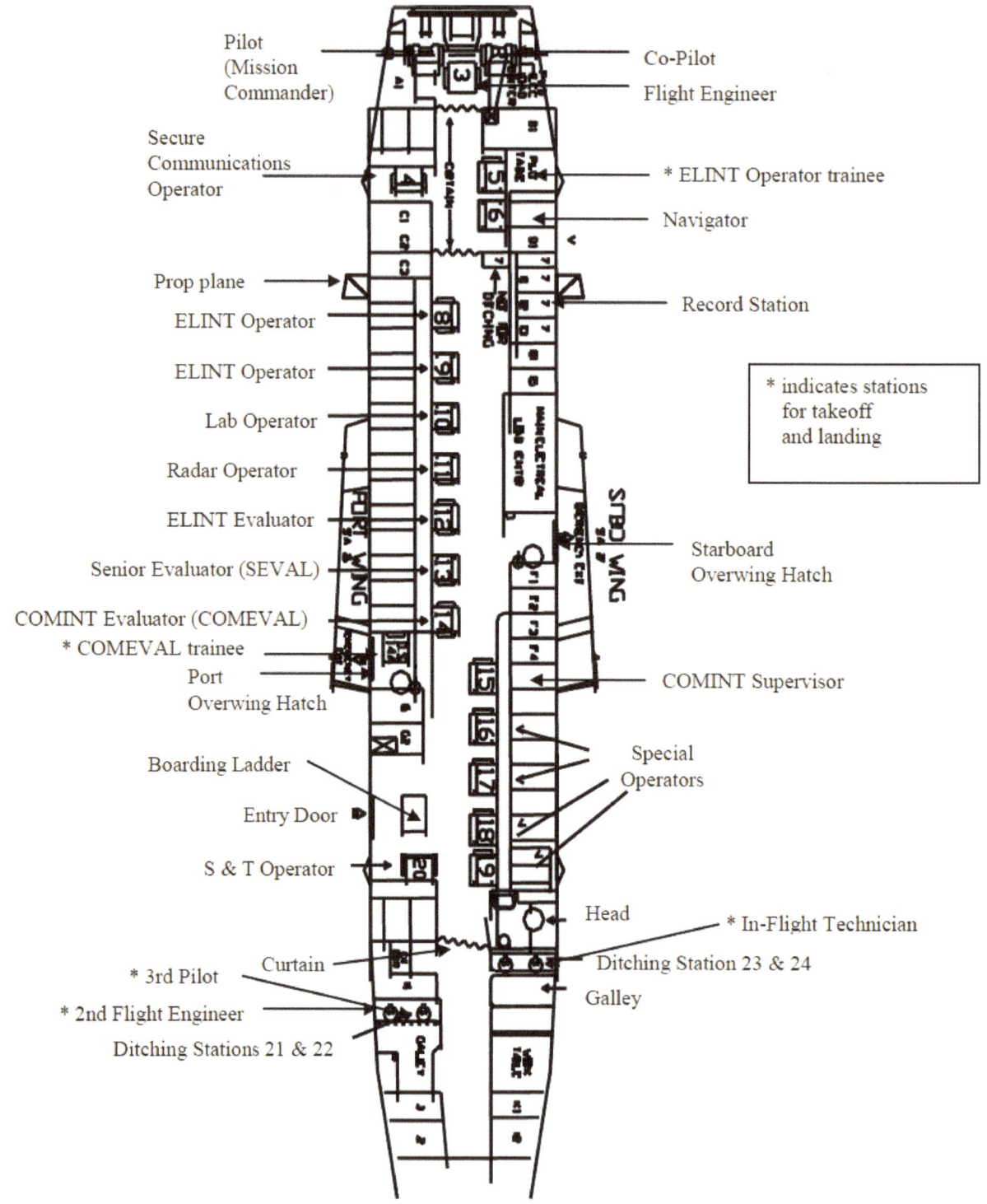

TOP SECRET//COMINT//NOFORN//X1

TOP SECRET//COMINT//NOFORN//X1

Appendix G

(U) Other Tactical SIGINT Platforms

(S//SI) EP-3 Cryptologic Assessment Team members visited several locations to gather data from other tactical SIGINT collection platforms and activities concerning their material accounting and destruction procedures. The visits focused on gaining insights into best practices for risk mitigation in the day-to-day conduct of tactical intelligence, surveillance and reconnaissance (ISR) missions. Units visited included: U.S. Air Force RC-135 COBRA BALL/COMBAT SENT/RIVET JOINT (Offutt AFB, NE); U.S. Army RC-7 ARL (Ft Bliss, TX); U.S. naval surface and subsurface assets (Norfolk Naval Base, VA); U.S. Air Force Special Operations assets (Hurlburt Field, FL), U.S. Army Special Operations assets (Ft Bragg, NC); and U.S. Marine Corps assets (Camp Lejeune, NC).

(U) RC-7 (U.S. Army)

(S) RC-7 Airborne Reconnaissance Low (ARL) mission aircraft include ARL Communications (ARL-C) and ARL Multifunction (ARL-M) variants. ARL missions are conducted in threat environment similar to that of the EP-3E. ARL mission crews employ Emergency Destruction Procedures (EDP) developed specifically for each aircraft configuration. The focus of these procedures is to mitigate potential loss of classified information in the event of an emergency landing.

(U//FOUO) The RC-7 Mission Supervisor (MS) is the designated authority for determining mission essential materials and inventories all mission materials brought onboard. The MS inventories the mission materials again after returning to the SCIF from the mission aircraft. A copy of the inventory is kept in the Mission Operations area IAW USSID 3.

(S) ARL collection operators are assigned consistent emergency destruction areas of responsibility based on assigned positions. Prior to each mission, the MS addresses individual rules of engagement and EDP areas of responsibility. Supervision of the EDP is the responsibility of the non-rated Mission Supervisor IAW the Mission Supervisors' Checklist for the particular mission aircraft. The MS EDP checklist is accessible at every position. When the EDP execution command is given, each operator complies with his/her responsibilities as listed in their individual checklist. When respective actions are completed, each operator informs the MS, who is responsible for notifying the flight deck.

(U) RC-135 (U.S. Air Force)

(U//FOUO) RC-135 aircraft conduct operations similar to the EP-3E, on JCS-approved SRO tracks. There are 21 total RC-135's in three variants: RIVET JOINT, with a primary SIGINT mission; COMBAT SENT, with a primary technical ELINT mission; and COBRA BALL, with a primary FISINT mission. All platforms carry

TOP SECRET//COMINT//NOFORN//X1

TOP SECRET//COMINT//NOFORN//X1

Sensitive Compartmented Information (SCI) data. Due to the proximity of these missions to unfriendly territory, RC-135 mission crews must carry out EDP in the event of aircraft loss, force down or damage. Emergency Destruction is ordered by the pilot (aircraft commander), lead electronic warfare officer (tactical controller (TC)), or airborne mission supervisor (AMS). Once destruction is initiated, aircrew members use their position checklists, which identify their respective responsibilities. Air Intelligence Agency (AIA) personnel (COMINT operators and COMINT systems maintenance) receive EDP familiarization during operator upgrade training. The Air Combat Command (ACC) personnel (pilots, navigators and electronic warfare officers) do not receive any standard EDP training.

(U//FOUO) Accountability for RC-135 mission materials is rigorous. For the COMINT compartment, the AMS verifies the inventory, signs a material receipt and files copies IAW USSID 3. After the mission, the materials are inventoried once by the AMS prior to departing the aircraft and again by the ground personnel when the materials are dropped off at the SCIF. CAT III materials may also be included on the mission inventory, but only if the AMS agrees they are required for the mission. For the ELINT compartment, the TC inventories and signs for the mission materials three times: prior to departure, before deplaning after the mission, and again when the materials are returned to the SCIF. ACC materials are generally non-SCI in nature.

(U//FOUO) RC-135 EDP is divided into two phases: preliminary and complete. During preliminary destruction, all non-essential materials (e.g., back-up discs, technical orders, tapes that have been recorded on) are destroyed. Hardcopy paper material is torn into small pieces and placed into any available containers in preparation for jettisoning. During complete destruction, the AMS executes a software command to initiate a disk overwrite process for all disks loaded in drives. Other crewmembers zeroize cryptographic equipment. Shredded paper material is jettisoned from the mission aircraft via the safest available window/hatch during complete destruction. Throughout EDP, crewmembers adhere to strict crew coordination standards. The AMS reports verbally over the aircraft intercom system to the TC and AC as each step of destruction is completed. Safety of the aircrew takes precedence over emergency destruction IAW Air Force Instruction (AFI) 11-202 Volume 3.

(C) A problem with the disk overwrite process is that it takes approximately three hours to complete. The goal is to decrease the time to less than 30 minutes.

(C) EDP is briefed prior to each mission. Each crewmember is directed to review their position checklist to become familiar with tasked responsibilities. Completion of survival courses, including special survival training (SV-83) geared towards unplanned detention situations, is mandatory for all RC-135 crewmembers. Furthermore, all COMINT crewmembers are tested in Advisory Support and Emergency Procedures every six months. EDP drills are not conducted prior to launch nor while airborne. Finally, the AIA has minimized classified paper holdings in favor of media storage.

TOP SECRET//COMINT//NOFORN//X1

(U) U.S. Air Force Special Operations Command (AFSOC) Standard Procedures

(C) AFSOC uses a Direct Support Operator (DSO) to provide direct threat warning to the supported aircrew. The DSO is normally the only SCI-indoctrinated aircrew member on AFSOC aircraft. The DSO carries a standard complement of materials, which are minimized by the station commander IAW USSID 3. The DSO accounts for and signs for sensitive equipment, which includes one UNCLASSIFIED, and one SECRET laptop. Additionally, the DSO carries a crypto storage device and one technical working aid, which is limited to SECRET information on water-soluble paper.

(S) Although the support afforded by the DSO includes an SCI collection and analysis process, no SCI data is actually placed in soft or hard copy materials. Also, only sanitized SECRET reporting is passed from the DSO to the supported crew.

(C) In an emergency situation, the DSO zeroizes all crypto devices, clears his laptop computers, destroys the hard drives of both laptops using a 9MM handgun or an axe, and adds water to the water soluble papers of the technical working aid.

(U) U.S. Army Special Operations Command (USASOC) Standard Procedures

(C) USASOC subordinated Special Forces Group (SFG) SIGINT assets deploy forward to provide threat warning for force protection of SFG elements. Collection elements deploy as a 5-person foot patrol team and all intercept equipment and associated materials are hauled via backpack. As such, they employ a "less is best" configuration and minimize crypto and technical data loads. Special Operation Team Bravo (SOT-B) teams establish a Tactical SCIF (T-SCIF) well behind the front line of defense. SOT-B T-SCIF authorities carry only the minimum crypto, tech data, and hard copy materials necessary for the mission at hand. Collection team leaders and T-SCIF Special Security Officers (SSO) are the designated authorities to monitor classified holdings and are responsible for minimizing classified materials.

(U//FOUO) When enemy contact is probable, team members zeroize all non-essential equipment (radios and crypto), destroy classified material and initiate egress operations. The preferred method for rapid destruction is thermite grenade.

(U) U.S. Marine Corps Standard Procedures

(S) The Marine Expeditionary Forces (MEF) employ Radio Battalions (RADBN) to conduct SIGINT operations to provide direct threat warning for force protection. RADBN personnel use a variety of configurations in both vehicle- and foot-based operations. Radio equipment is tailored to the specific mission and technical data is minimized due to operations in close proximity to enemy lines. SCI used by forward teams is normally limited to one cheat sheet and team leaders, as the designated deployed authority, prefer that these sheets be sanitized to the collateral SECRET level. A copy of mission material inventories is left at the headquarters location. The RADBN commander has overall authority to determine materials brought on a deployment.

TOP SECRET//COMINT//NOFORN//X1

TOP SECRET//COMINT//NOFORN//X1

(U//FOUO) When High Mobility Wheeled Vehicles (HMMWVs) are used, they are configured for the particular mission and the teams carry minimal crypto, technical data and hard copy materials. Radio Reconnaissance Teams (RRTs) travel on foot and use backpacks for all intercept equipment and associated materials. As such, they employ a "less is best" configuration. During ship borne operations, the RADBN personnel team with U.S. Navy operators and follow the applicable EAP for the respective ship.

(U//FOUO) If enemy contact is probable, team members zeroize all non-essential equipment (radios and crypto) while executing egress operations. If enemy attack is imminent, then all classified equipment, to include the vehicle would be destroyed using thermite grenades.

(U) Naval Surface Vessel Standard Procedures

(S) All SCI material aboard U.S. Navy surface assets will be confined to authorized areas. For augmenting cryptologic personnel, the Operations Officer of the supporting Naval Security Group Activity (NSGA) determines what mission materials can be deployed. Additionally, the ship's Commanding Officer (CO) can place limits on the materials embarked.

(U//FOUO) If the situation warrants, the ship's CO or his/her designee will direct activation of the EDP. The EDP is conducted in three phases: preliminary destruction, precautionary destruction, and total destruction. Destruction procedures are outlined on EDP cards, maintained at the watch officer desk. The cards are passed out to duty personnel, who follow the prioritized destruction guidelines.

(U//FOUO) The ship's CMS Custodian is responsible for reviewing EDP cards periodically and for ensuring that appropriate emergency destruction tools are available and serviceable.

(U) Naval Subsurface Standard Procedures

(S) U.S. Navy subsurface assets may or may not embark an NSG SIGINT collection contingent. When NSG personnel participate in subsurface operations, the Operations Officer of the supporting NSGA determines what mission materials can be deployed. Due to extremely limited space considerations, the submarine CO may further restrict materials brought onboard. Submarine operations are generally confined to a smaller operations area, facilitating a more condensed SCI material inventory for mission accomplishment. An inventory of supporting NSGA SCI materials is maintained at their respective units.

(U//FOUO) If the situation warrants, the Commanding Officer or his designee will direct activation of the EDP. NSGA personnel will destroy their materials using shredders, axes, and sledgehammers, where appropriate.

TOP SECRET//COMINT//NOFORN//X1

Appendix H

(U) Crisis Response Interviews

(U//FOUO) Team members conducted interviews with the following individuals.

NSA	NSOC Chief, ████
	NSOC D/Chief, ████
	SSA, LtCol ████ USMC
	SID/DDAP, ████
	SID/Chief, Office of China, ████ (Crisis Manager)
	SID/Chief, China Military Division, ████ (Chair, CMSG)
	SOO, ████
	NSOC C/S, ████ (EP-3 desk)
	NSOC Dep C/S, ████ (EP-3 desk)
	SID/DDDA - ████
	SID/Reporting Policy, ████
	SID/Office of China, Reporting Policy, ████
	LAO, ████
	PAO, ████
PACOM	CINCPAC Dep J2, ████ USA
	CINCPAC J28, ████
	CINCPACFLT N2, ████
	CINCPACFLT N3DC, ████
	Joint Recce Center, ████
	Joint Recce Center ████
	J284, Collection Operations, ████
	NCPAC, Charlie Meals
	NCPAC Ops Chief, ████
	NCPAC IAD Chief, ████
	CSG Hawaii, ████
KRSOC	Commander, ████ USN
	Dep C/S, ████
	J3, LtCol ██z, USAF
	J3 OPS, LT ████
State	Acting A/S for INR, ████
	DAS for INR, ████
	State/INR, ████ Asia Desk
	State/INR, ████
	State/INR, ████
	NCR State, ████

TOP SECRET//COMINT//NOFORN//X1

TOP SECRET//COMINT//NOFORN//X1

Pentagon   JCS J2, RADM ▮
                JCS J2M, CAPT ▮
                DUSD(PS), ▮
                DNI, RADM P▮
                NCR Defense, ▮
                CSG, ▮
                J38, Col ▮ USAF

White House   NSC Intel Director, ▮
                      Deputy Director, Situation Room, ▮

CIA   DDCI MA, Lt Gen ▮
        ADCI Collection, ▮
        D/ADCI Anal & Prod, ▮

Congress   ▮, SSCI
              ▮, HPSCI
              ▮, HPSCI
              ▮ HPSCI

TOP SECRET//COMINT//NOFORN//X1

Appendix I

(U//FOUO) EP-3 Cryptologic Assessment Team Members

Co-Leads

▮▮▮▮▮▮▮▮	NSA
CAPT ▮▮▮▮▮, USN	NSG

Members

LT ▮▮▮▮▮, USN	ONI
CTA2 ▮▮▮▮▮ USN	NSG
Lt Col ▮▮▮▮▮, USAF	NSA
▮▮▮▮▮	NSA
▮▮▮▮▮	INSCOM
▮▮▮▮▮	NSA
▮▮▮▮▮	NSA
LCDR ▮▮▮▮▮, USN	Patrol and Reconnaissance Wing TEN
▮▮▮▮▮	NSA
SMSGT ▮▮▮▮▮, USAF	AFCO
▮▮▮▮▮	NSA
▮▮▮▮▮	NSA
LT ▮▮▮▮▮, USN	NSG

Oversight

RADM ▮▮▮▮▮ USN	Commander, NSG

TOP SECRET//COMINT//NOFORN//X1

TOP SECRET//COMINT//NOFORN//X1

Appendix J

(U) EP-3 Incident Assessment and Review
Terms of Reference

4 May 2001

1. (U//FOUO) **Executive Issue**

   ➢ This document outlines the Terms of Reference for a SIGINT and Information Assurance damage assessment and incident review of the EP-3E/F-8-II collision on 1 April 2001, as directed by the Chief, Naval Operations (CNO) and the Director, National Security Agency/Chief, Central Security Service (DIRNSA).

2. (U//FOUO) **Background**

   ➢ The collision incident requires a comprehensive, fully coordinated, end-to-end damage assessment, including a review of emergency procedures and actions, development of lessons learned, and recommendations for corrective action, where appropriate.

3. (S//SI) **Overview**

   ➢ *Structure*. Overall incident assessment and review to be conducted at COMNAVSECGRU HQ, Fort Meade, MD by a multi-organizational team co-chaired by Navy and the National Security Agency (NSA). The EP-3 Cryptologic Assessment Team will be comprised of two working groups. Group One will be led by NSA and tasked with conducting damage assessment and review of the Cryptologic system response and procedures. Group two will be led by the Navy and tasked with review and assessment of emergency destruction, classified material accountability, communications and connectivity and emergency procedures.
   ➢ *Membership*. Members will be both core and extended. Core members will be detailed to the working groups for the duration of the assessment. Extended members will interface virtually or in person as appropriate. COMNAVSECGRU will oversee the effort on behalf of the CNO and the DIRNSA.
   ➢ *Final Report*. The team will produce a final report including an incident summary, a complete list of what was compromised and the impact of that loss, lessons learned, and near-, mid-, and long-term recommendations for improvement to include proposed action agencies and timelines. The team will update COMNAVSECGRU on at least a weekly basis and will provide Congress, Defense, and Intelligence Community components updates as required.

TOP SECRET//COMINT//NOFORN//X1

TOP SECRET//COMINT//NOFORN//X1

4. (S//SI) **Working Groups**

> ➢ Working Group composition and focus areas.

Group 1A Lead: NSA (SIGINT Directorate)

Tasking: SIGINT damage assessment and review of SIGINT system crisis response
Members: NSA (SID), Navy, CINCPAC, NCPAC, KRSOC, Service Cryptologic Elements (SCEs)
Focus Areas:
  (1) SIGINT Equipment and Techniques: Loss and damage
  (2) SIGINT technical information exposure: Loss and damage
  (3) Crisis response procedures
  (4) Communications/connectivity
  (5) Information management and dissemination
  (6) Cross-organization and agency coordination
  (7) Foreign partner impacts
  (8) Damage Mitigation
  (9) Collection/analysis strategy to confirm loss/damage assessment, including initial observations of target activities

Group 1B Lead: NSA (IA Directorate)

Tasking: IA damage assessment and review of Cryptologic Material System (CMS) equipment, medium protection capabilities, and procedures.
Members: NSA (IAD), SCEs
Focus Areas:
  (1) IA information: Loss and damage
  (2) Technical information: Loss and damage
  (3) Crisis response procedures
  (4) Information management and dissemination
  (5) Cross-organization and agency coordination
  (6) Damage mitigation
  (7) Collection/analysis strategy to confirm loss/damage assessment

Group 2 Lead: Navy

Tasking: Review emergency destruction, Classified material accountability and documentation, communications and connectivity (internal/external), and emergency procedures.
Members: Navy (OPNAV, CINCPAC, CINPACFLT, ONI), NSA(SID/IAD), NAVAIR, COMPATRECONFORPAC, SCEs
Focus Areas:
  (1) Classified Material Accountability and Documentation

TOP SECRET//COMINT//NOFORN//X1

TOP SECRET//COMINT//NOFORN//X1

- Requirements
- Procedures (accountability/control)
- Equipment
- Hardcopy material
- Softcopy material
- Configuration management

(2) Emergency Destruction
- Requirements
- Procedures (priorities, methods, tools, equipment)
- Equipment and capabilities
- Technical improvements and requirements for future systems

(3) Communications and connectivity

(4) Emergency Procedures
- Flights
- SRO
- NATOPS
- Aircrew coordination

5. (U) Interim Deliverables

- Outline of Report (to CNO and DIRNSA).
- Weekly feedback and periodic status reports (CNO, CINCPAC, CINCPACFLT, DIRNSA, DOD, and the Intelligence Community).

6. (U//FOUO) Final Report

- The final report, with an Executive Summary and briefing, will be delivered to the CNO and DIRNSA. It will include a:
  - Summary of the incident from collision to repatriation
  - Damage assessment of SIGINT and IA equipment, techniques, and information compromised
  - Review and assessment of operational activities
  - Counterintelligence assessment
  - Review of SIGINT and IA crisis response
  - Consolidated lessons learned and near-, mid-, and long-term recommendations, including action agencies and deliverable timelines

7. (U//FOUO) Timeline Milestones

- Official start of Assessment Team — 27 April
- Draft and coordinate Terms of Reference — 27 April
- Data gathering, to include TDY for crew debriefs — 27 April -1 June

TOP SECRET//COMINT//NOFORN//X1

TOP SECRET//COMINT//NOFORN//X1

➢ Release final Terms of Reference	4 May
➢ Release outline of report	11 May
➢ Integration of team inputs, drafting of final report	4-19 June
➢ Release draft final report for coordination, review	20 June
➢ Brief CNO and DIRNSA on report	Week of 25 June
➢ Final report issued; Team stand down	12 July

8. (U//FOUO) **Considerations**

- ➢ Team/group composition must balanced in size and expertise.
- ➢ Information must be managed to avoid premature disclosure and to protect the fact finding process.
- ➢ "Protected" lists of authorized recipients will be created to guide dissemination for each team and overall assessment. Release of information beyond the list of authorized recipients will be controlled by CNO and DIRNSA.
- ➢ Follow-on information requirements for the EP-3E crew can be anticipated.

www.ingramcontent.com/pod-product-compliance
Lightning Source LLC
Chambersburg PA
CBHW082124230426
43671CB00015B/2801